# Table of Contents

*This lesson plan book belongs to:*

Name _______________________________

School _______________________________

Grade/Subject _______________________________

Room _______________________________

School Year _______________________________

Address _______________________________

Phone _______________________________

**Teacher Created Reasources, Inc.**
6421 Industry Way
Westminster, CA  92683
www.teachercreated.com

**ISBN:  978-0-7439-7028-0**

©2003 Teacher Created Resourcers, Inc.
Reprinted, 2010
Made in U.S.A.

**Project Manager:**  Lorin Klistoff, M.A.
**Cover Art:**  Brenda DiAntonis
**Imaging:**  James Edward Grace

# Ways to Use This Book

### Seating Chart (Page 3)

A seating chart is provided for easy reference. Table or desk arrangement will vary throughout the year depending on room size, available furniture, grade level taught, teaching style, and academic program needs. To accommodate a variety of classroom arrangements, you may wish to create additional charts and place specific seating information in a separate folder.

### Student Roster (Pages 4 and 5)

Record both student and parent or guardian names and addresses. Make a special note of differences in last names when appropriate. You may wish to list siblings and their grades. Notes may include children with special needs or medications that are necessary.

### Blessed Birthdays (Page 6)

Write in the boxes names and birthdates of students. Identify each special day with a birthday greeting. Remind them how special they are to God, too. You can sing to them or present a special birthday hat.

### Weekly Schedule (Page 7)

If your schedule changes periodically, you may wish to duplicate this page before completing your current schedule. Attach new schedules throughout the year, as need arises.

### Year At a Glance (Pages 8 and 9)

Use this chart to plan units of study and/or focus on immediate and upcoming events, conferences, meetings, seminars, and other important dates. Record each event as soon as you are notified. The Year At a Glance chart can also be reproduced for students to help them plan projects and keep track of important dates and events.

### Substitute Teacher Information (Pages 10 and 11)

Record all pertinent information on these pages. If you have a copy of the layout of your school, attach it to this page; otherwise, sketch an outline of the school grounds, showing restrooms, office, lounge, playground, etc. Attach a paper clip to both this page and the lesson page for easy reference.

### Weekly Memory Verse (Pages 12 and 13)

Record your weekly memory verse on these pages. You can have all your memory verses together at a glance for all 40 weeks.

### Bulletin Board Ideas (Pages 14 and 15)

Use these bulletin boards ideas to enhance the classroom atmosphere! These colorful bulletin boards will grab student's attention and can teach and illustrate important Biblical concepts. Every bulletin board teaches a truth which can be applied to the student's life in a practical way.

### Quick Bible Activities (Pages 16)

Use some of these activities to enhance or supplement your curriculum. They can also be used as quick fillers in between subjects. Most activities come with scripture references.

### Class Records (Pages 17–76)

The class records section is designed to provide organized space for recording daily notations or grades for assignments, tests, attendance, tardies, participation, etc. Each page contains a five-week block of spaces so that a student's record for an entire quarter of ten weeks can be read on facing pages. A summary column for recording total attendance, tardies, and grades appear on the right-hand facing page for each ten-week period. Enough record sheets are provided to last for two 20-week semesters, accomodating seven different classes or preparations. Two extra pages of record sheets covering 10 weeks (or one quarter) are provided for copy or replacement purposes.

### Lesson Plans (Pages 77–160)

Use the lesson plans to help you organize yourself each week. There are enough weekly plan pages to cover a 40-week school year. At the top of the left-hand page, fill in the blank to indicate the week dates for which the plans are written. The last column may be used for notes or reminders. Also, read the Biblical verse in the top right-hand page to inspire you throughout the week!

# Seating Chart

## Seat Arrangement Ideas

Sticky notes can be used to temporarily assign seats.

### 1. Basic Row Seating

### 2. U-Shaped Seating

### 3. Rectangle

### 4. Partner Seating

The size and shape of your room will play a large part in your seating arrangement.

You may want to change this layout once you are familiar with your students and their needs.

Regardless of your seating plan, the most important concern is that you can easily see all your students and the children in turn have good visibility of you, the chalkboard, and other focal points in the room.

***Front of Classroom***

# Student Roster

| | Student | Parent/Guardian | Address |
|---|---|---|---|
| 1. | | | |
| 2. | | | |
| 3. | | | |
| 4. | | | |
| 5. | | | |
| 6. | | | |
| 7. | | | |
| 8. | | | |
| 9. | | | |
| 10. | | | |
| 11. | | | |
| 12. | | | |
| 13. | | | |
| 14. | | | |
| 15. | | | |
| 16. | | | |
| 17. | | | |
| 18. | | | |
| 19. | | | |
| 20. | | | |
| 21. | | | |
| 22. | | | |
| 23. | | | |
| 24. | | | |
| 25. | | | |
| 26. | | | |
| 27. | | | |
| 28. | | | |
| 29. | | | |
| 30. | | | |
| 31. | | | |
| 32. | | | |
| 33. | | | |
| 34. | | | |
| 35. | | | |
| 36. | | | |

# Student Roster

| Home & Work Phones | Birthday | Siblings | Notes |
| --- | --- | --- | --- |
|  |  |  |  |
|  |  |  |  |
|  |  |  |  |
|  |  |  |  |
|  |  |  |  |
|  |  |  |  |
|  |  |  |  |
|  |  |  |  |
|  |  |  |  |
|  |  |  |  |
|  |  |  |  |
|  |  |  |  |
|  |  |  |  |
|  |  |  |  |
|  |  |  |  |
|  |  |  |  |
|  |  |  |  |
|  |  |  |  |
|  |  |  |  |
|  |  |  |  |
|  |  |  |  |
|  |  |  |  |

# Blessed Birthdays

| August | September | October |
|---|---|---|
| | | |
| November | December | January |
| | | |
| February | March | April |
| | | |
| May | June | July |
| | | |

# Weekly Schedule

| Time | Monday | Tuesday | Wednesday | Thursday | Friday |
|---|---|---|---|---|---|
|  |  |  |  |  |  |
|  |  |  |  |  |  |
|  |  |  |  |  |  |
|  |  |  |  |  |  |
|  |  |  |  |  |  |
|  |  |  |  |  |  |
|  |  |  |  |  |  |
|  |  |  |  |  |  |
|  |  |  |  |  |  |
|  |  |  |  |  |  |
|  |  |  |  |  |  |
|  |  |  |  |  |  |

# Year At A Glance

| September | October |
| --- | --- |
|  |  |
| **January** | **February** |
|  |  |
| **May** | **June** |
|  |  |

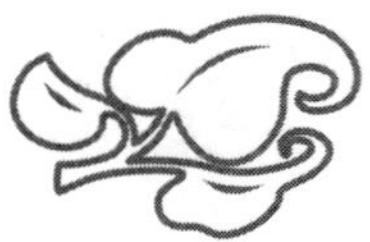

| November | December |
|---|---|
| | |
| **March** | **April** |
| | |
| **July** | **August** |
| | |

# Substitute Teacher Information

## School Schedule

- Class Begins _______________________________
- Morning Recess _____________________________
- Lunchtime _________________________________
- Class Resumes ______________________________
- Afternoon Recess ____________________________
- Dismissal _________________________________

## Special Notes

_____________________________________________
_____________________________________________
_____________________________________________
_____________________________________________
_____________________________________________
_____________________________________________
_____________________________________________
_____________________________________________

## Special Classes

Student _____________________________________

Class ______________ Day _________ Time _________

Student _____________________________________

Class ______________ Day _________ Time _________

Student _____________________________________

Class ______________ Day _________ Time _________

## Special Needs Students

| Student | Needs | Time and Place |
| --- | --- | --- |
| _____________ | _____________ | _____________ |
| _____________ | _____________ | _____________ |
| _____________ | _____________ | _____________ |
| _____________ | _____________ | _____________ |
| _____________ | _____________ | _____________ |
| _____________ | _____________ | _____________ |

## Where to Find

- Class List _________________________________
- School Layout ______________________________
- Seating Chart ______________________________
- Attendance Record ___________________________
- Lesson Plans _______________________________
- Teacher Manuals ____________________________
- First Aid Kit _______________________________
- Emergency Information _______________________
- Supplementary Activities _____________________
- Class Supplies–paper, pencils, etc. _____________
- Referral forms and procedures _______________

_____________________________________________
_____________________________________________
_____________________________________________
_____________________________________________
_____________________________________________
_____________________________________________
_____________________________________________
_____________________________________________
_____________________________________________
_____________________________________________
_____________________________________________
_____________________________________________

# Substitute Teacher Information

## Classroom Standards

- When finished with an assignment

  _________________________________________

  _________________________________________

- When and how to speak out in class

  _________________________________________

  _________________________________________

- Incentive Program

  _________________________________________

  _________________________________________

- Discipline

  _________________________________________

  _________________________________________

- Restroom Procedure

  _________________________________________

  _________________________________________

## People Who Can Help

- Teacher/Room _______________________________

- Dependable Students _______________________

  _________________________________________

  _________________________________________

  _________________________________________

  _________________________________________

  _________________________________________

- Principal _________________________________

- Secretary _________________________________

- Custodian _________________________________

- Counselor _________________________________

- Nurse _____________________________________

***Layout of School***—including school office, faculty lounge, restrooms, auditorium, playground, etc. (or attach printed diagram here)

# Weekly Memory Verse

Week of: _______________________
Verse: _________________________
_______________________________

Week of: _______________________
Verse: _________________________
_______________________________

Week of: _______________________
Verse: _________________________
_______________________________

Week of: _______________________
Verse: _________________________
_______________________________

Week of: _______________________
Verse: _________________________
_______________________________

Week of: _______________________
Verse: _________________________
_______________________________

Week of: _______________________
Verse: _________________________
_______________________________

Week of: _______________________
Verse: _________________________
_______________________________

Week of: _______________________
Verse: _________________________
_______________________________

Week of: _______________________
Verse: _________________________
_______________________________

Week of: _______________________
Verse: _________________________
_______________________________

Week of: _______________________
Verse: _________________________
_______________________________

Week of: _______________________
Verse: _________________________
_______________________________

Week of: _______________________
Verse: _________________________
_______________________________

Week of: _______________________
Verse: _________________________
_______________________________

Week of: _______________________
Verse: _________________________
_______________________________

Week of: _______________________
Verse: _________________________
_______________________________

Week of: _______________________
Verse: _________________________
_______________________________

# Weekly Memory Verse

Week of: ___________________________
Verse: _____________________________
__________________________________

Week of: ___________________________
Verse: _____________________________
__________________________________

Week of: ___________________________
Verse: _____________________________
__________________________________

Week of: ___________________________
Verse: _____________________________
__________________________________

Week of: ___________________________
Verse: _____________________________
__________________________________

Week of: ___________________________
Verse: _____________________________
__________________________________

Week of: ___________________________
Verse: _____________________________
__________________________________

Week of: ___________________________
Verse: _____________________________
__________________________________

Week of: ___________________________
Verse: _____________________________
__________________________________

Week of: ___________________________
Verse: _____________________________

Week of: ___________________________
Verse: _____________________________
__________________________________

Week of: ___________________________
Verse: _____________________________
__________________________________

Week of: ___________________________
Verse: _____________________________
__________________________________

Week of: ___________________________
Verse: _____________________________
__________________________________

Week of: ___________________________
Verse: _____________________________
__________________________________

Week of: ___________________________
Verse: _____________________________
__________________________________

Week of: ___________________________
Verse: _____________________________
__________________________________

Week of: ___________________________
Verse: _____________________________
__________________________________

Week of: ___________________________
Verse: _____________________________

# Bulletin Board Ideas

Use these bulletin boards ideas to enhance the classroom atmosphere!  These colorful bulletin boards will grab student's attention and can teach and illustrate important Biblical concepts.  Every bulletin board teaches a truth which can be applied to the student's life in a practical way.

### Why Did Jesus Die?

Cover the bulletin board with black paper.  Cut a large cross from light brown paper and attach it to the center of the board.  Write the following question on red paper:  "Why Did Jesus Die?" and attach it above the cross.  Write the following answer on a large yellow strip of paper, "To Take the Punishment for My Sins."  Mount the answer below the cross.  Then give each student a cut-out red paper heart.  Have students write short thank-you notes to Jesus on the hearts and attach them to the board around the cross.

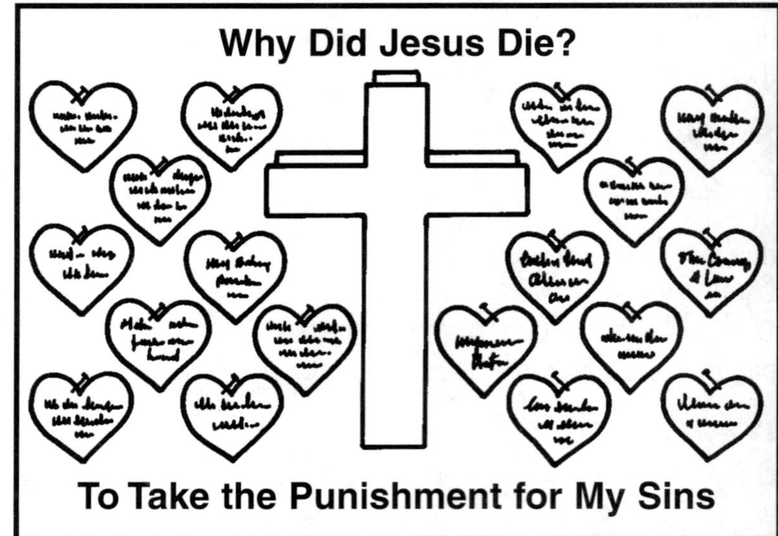



### Follow the Son!

Cover the board with blue paper.  Print the caption "Follow the Son!" and the saying "He provides us with everything for our enjoyment!" (I Timothy 6:17) on strips of yellow paper.  Place the caption at the top of the board and the verse on the bottom of the board.  Cut a large, yellow sun out of yellow paper and mount it on the board.  Enlarge a figure of Jesus and place it on the sun.  Have children bring photos and postcards from past summers and attach them to the board.

### Promises You Can Be-"leave"

Cover the board with blue paper.  Print the caption "Promises You Can Be-'leave'" on piece of construction paper.  Cut leaf shapes from colored paper and print Bible promises on them, such as Genesis 8:22, Joshua 1:5, Psalm 55:22, Jeremiah 33:3a, Matthew 11:28, John 3:16, John 14:2, Phillipians 4:19, and your own choices.  Scatter the leaves over the board.  Let children bring in real leaves from their yards and add them to the board.

### When Should I Pray?

Cover the board with light green paper.  Use a black marker to print the question "When Should I Pray?" across the top of the board.  Print the word "Anytime" at the bottom of the board.  Print the following captions with a simple face drawing:  "first thing in the morning" (face yawning), "last thing at night" (face is sleeping), "at mealtime" (face with tongue sticking out), "when I feel scared" (face showing anxiety), and "when I am happy" (face smiling).  Attach the captions and drawings on the board.

### All Creatures Great and Small

Cover the board with bright blue paper.  Print the caption "All Creatures Great and Small, The Lord God Made Them All!" on yellow paper and mount it at the top of the board.  Then print the Bible verses ("Ask the animals, and they will teach you . . . In his hand is the life of every creature." Job 12:7, 10) on yellow paper and mount them at the bottom of the board.  Let children look through nature magazines for animals of all kinds, cut them out, and add them to the center of the board.

# Bulletin Board Ideas

### God Is With Me

Cover the board with dark green paper. Print the caption "Wherever I Go, God Is With Me" on a light green strip of paper. Place it at the top of the board. Print "God is our refuge and strength, an ever-present help in trouble." (Psalm 46:1) on a light green strip of paper and mount it at the bottom of the board. Have students bring photos of themselves in various places doing different things: family vacation, asleep, eating, etc. Place the photos all over the board.

### Jesus Is the Bridge

Cover the board with blue paper. Print the caption "Jesus Is the Bridge From Earth to Heaven" on a white strip of paper. Mount the caption on the top of the board. Use a black marker to draw a simple bridge spanning the distance between two masses of land. Label the two masses of land as "Earth" and "Heaven," "Sin" and "Salvation," or "Death" and "Life." Label the bridge "Jesus." Print Jesus' statement in John 14:6, "Jesus said, 'I am the way and the truth and the life. No one comes to the Father except through me,'" on the background paper or on a paper strip and attach under the bridge.

### Praise God

Cover the board with red paper. Cut the following letters very large from white paper: P, R, A, I, S, E, G, O, D. Use red marker to print "Let everything that has breath praise the Lord!" (Psalm 150:6) on a strip of white paper and attach it to the bottom of the board. Lay the large, white letters on a table. Let students use red and black markers to write words of praise to God on the letters. Emphasize to everyone the need to work carefully so as to not bend or tear the letters. Mount the large letters on the board.

### Heaven

Cover the board with blue paper. Print the question "What's So Great About Heaven?" on a white strip of paper. Mount it across the top of the board. Cut seven cloud shapes from white paper. On each cloud print the following captions and verse references: "No Sin" (Revelation 21:27), "Jesus" (John 14:2), "No Night" (Revelation 21:25), "No Death" (Revelation 21:4), "A Place for Me Prepared by Jesus" (John 14:3), "No Pain" (Revelation 21:4), "Streets of Gold" (Revelation 21:21). Glue cotton around the edges of the clouds. Scatter the clouds on the board.

### Our Powerful God

Cover the board with black paper. Cut letters for the caption "Our Powerful God" from gold or silver paper and mount it at the top of the board. Print 2 Chronicles 20:6 on a large cloud cut-out and put it at the center of the board. Ask students to write or draw a time when they seen God's power in their life. If they cannot think of any ideas, have them go through the Bible and display a story that exhibits God's power, such as the flood or the healing of the lame man. Post their drawings or writings around the cloud.

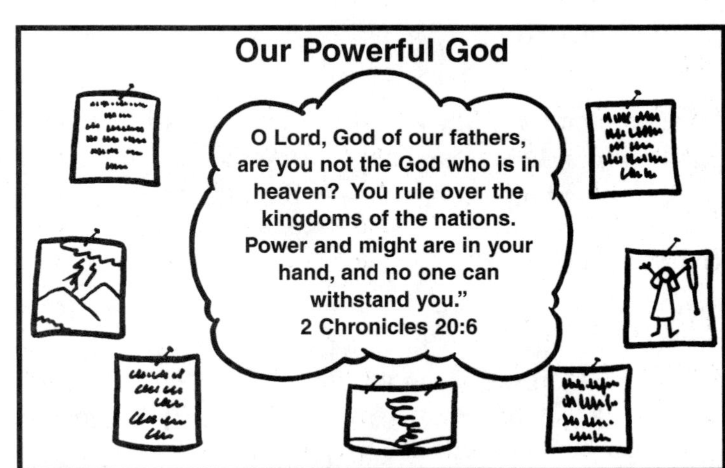

# Quick Bible Activities

Building Christian character in students is an important task. The activities below are a quick and easy way to achieve such a goal. The activities are great ways to get students into the habit of praising and honoring God.

### Count Your Blessings

Hand each child a piece of notebook paper. Tell the children that they are going to have a contest to see who can list the most blessings from God. They must all begin at the same time and end at whatever time limit you set. Then have them count how many blessings each one listed. Let the winner read his or her list to the class first. If time allows, let the other students read their lists. Then have a moment of silent prayer, allowing the students to thank God for everything on their lists.

### Role-Playing

Read the story of Jonah in Jonah 1–3. Talk about how Jonah was sorry about running away from what the Lord told him to do. Then divide the class into small groups or pairs. Tell each group that they will given a few minutes to work up a simple skit to perform to the class. Each skit should be about a situation in which someone does something wrong and then says, " I'm sorry."

### Job Charades

Read Genesis 37, 39, 41, and 45. Talk about how Joseph was responsible for many important things. Ahead of time, write down a list of occupations on a piece of paper (for example:  doctor, teacher, car mechanic, secretary, farmer, pilot, soldier, dentist, etc.). Make sure there is one per child. Cut the list into strips, and put them in a cup. Have the students take turns drawing out a strip and acting out the job. Tell them to act out the responsibilities that someone with that job would have. The others can guess what kind of worker is being acted out.

### Prayer Journal

Give each student several sheets of 8½" x 11" paper to cut in half. Have students assemble their pages together. Staple the pages together to make a journal book. Have them label the cover "My Prayer Journal" and write their name on it. Ask students to decorate the cover. Discuss the best way to use a prayer journal. Explain that a journal is a good way to remember prayer requests and to make a note of when and how God answers each prayer. Periodically, ask volunteers to share some of their contents of their prayer journals.

### Helping Hands

Read I Corinthians 4:12 and discuss the verse. Explain that God gave us helping hands so we can help others. Have students trace their hands on white paper and cut them out. On each hand, have students write one way that they will help somebody during the day or week. When they have achieved the task, mount their hand in a book or on a bulletin board with the title, "God's Helping Hands."

### Tell the Truth

Read Acts 4:32–35 and 5:1–11. Discuss what happened to Ananias and Sapphira when they did not tell the truth. Then have the students put their chairs in a circle, or sit in a circle on the floor. Tell them that they are going to take turns going around the circle. The students must take turns saying their names and then telling one true thing about themselves using the first letter of their names. For example, "My name is Jamie, and I like to jump rope," or "My name is Scott, and I like to swim." Tell the students to try and remember what every child says because when everyone is finished, the game will be played again in a different way. This time, however, each child must say the name of the student to his or her right and what was true about him or her. Even if the player cannot remember, he or she must guess. If the student remembers the true thing, he or she stays in the game. If he or she says something false, he or she is out.

# Class Records

*If you, O Lord, kept a record of sins,*

*who could stand?*

*Psalm 130:3*

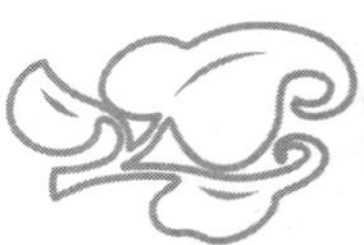

# $\mathcal{S}$ubject______________________

| Week | Week____ | | | | | Week____ | | | | | Week____ | | | | | Week____ | | | | | Week____ | | | | |
|---|---|---|---|---|---|---|---|---|---|---|---|---|---|---|---|---|---|---|---|---|---|---|---|---|---|
| Day | M | T | W | T | F | M | T | W | T | F | M | T | W | T | F | M | T | W | T | F | M | T | W | T | F |
| Date | | | | | | | | | | | | | | | | | | | | | | | | | |
| Assignments or Attendance | | | | | | | | | | | | | | | | | | | | | | | | | |
| Name | | | | | | | | | | | | | | | | | | | | | | | | | |
| 1 | | | | | | | | | | | | | | | | | | | | | | | | | |
| 2 | | | | | | | | | | | | | | | | | | | | | | | | | |
| 3 | | | | | | | | | | | | | | | | | | | | | | | | | |
| 4 | | | | | | | | | | | | | | | | | | | | | | | | | |
| 5 | | | | | | | | | | | | | | | | | | | | | | | | | |
| 6 | | | | | | | | | | | | | | | | | | | | | | | | | |
| 7 | | | | | | | | | | | | | | | | | | | | | | | | | |
| 8 | | | | | | | | | | | | | | | | | | | | | | | | | |
| 9 | | | | | | | | | | | | | | | | | | | | | | | | | |
| 10 | | | | | | | | | | | | | | | | | | | | | | | | | |
| 11 | | | | | | | | | | | | | | | | | | | | | | | | | |
| 12 | | | | | | | | | | | | | | | | | | | | | | | | | |
| 13 | | | | | | | | | | | | | | | | | | | | | | | | | |
| 14 | | | | | | | | | | | | | | | | | | | | | | | | | |
| 15 | | | | | | | | | | | | | | | | | | | | | | | | | |
| 16 | | | | | | | | | | | | | | | | | | | | | | | | | |
| 17 | | | | | | | | | | | | | | | | | | | | | | | | | |
| 18 | | | | | | | | | | | | | | | | | | | | | | | | | |
| 19 | | | | | | | | | | | | | | | | | | | | | | | | | |
| 20 | | | | | | | | | | | | | | | | | | | | | | | | | |
| 21 | | | | | | | | | | | | | | | | | | | | | | | | | |
| 22 | | | | | | | | | | | | | | | | | | | | | | | | | |
| 23 | | | | | | | | | | | | | | | | | | | | | | | | | |
| 24 | | | | | | | | | | | | | | | | | | | | | | | | | |
| 25 | | | | | | | | | | | | | | | | | | | | | | | | | |
| 26 | | | | | | | | | | | | | | | | | | | | | | | | | |
| 27 | | | | | | | | | | | | | | | | | | | | | | | | | |
| 28 | | | | | | | | | | | | | | | | | | | | | | | | | |
| 29 | | | | | | | | | | | | | | | | | | | | | | | | | |
| 30 | | | | | | | | | | | | | | | | | | | | | | | | | |
| 31 | | | | | | | | | | | | | | | | | | | | | | | | | |
| 32 | | | | | | | | | | | | | | | | | | | | | | | | | |
| 33 | | | | | | | | | | | | | | | | | | | | | | | | | |
| 34 | | | | | | | | | | | | | | | | | | | | | | | | | |
| 35 | | | | | | | | | | | | | | | | | | | | | | | | | |
| 36 | | | | | | | | | | | | | | | | | | | | | | | | | |

# *Period*____________________

| Week____ | | | | | Week____ | | | | | Week____ | | | | | Week____ | | | | | Week____ | | | | | | *Days Present* | *Days Absent* | *Tardies* | *Quarter Grade* | |
|---|---|---|---|---|---|---|---|---|---|---|---|---|---|---|---|---|---|---|---|---|---|---|---|---|---|---|---|---|---|---|---|
| M | T | W | T | F | M | T | W | T | F | M | T | W | T | F | M | T | W | T | F | M | T | W | T | F | | | | | | |
| | | | | | | | | | | | | | | | | | | | | | | | | | | | | | | |
| | | | | | | | | | | | | | | | | | | | | | | | | | | | | | | |
| | | | | | | | | | | | | | | | | | | | | | | | | | 1 | | | | | |
| | | | | | | | | | | | | | | | | | | | | | | | | | 2 | | | | | |
| | | | | | | | | | | | | | | | | | | | | | | | | | 3 | | | | | |
| | | | | | | | | | | | | | | | | | | | | | | | | | 4 | | | | | |
| | | | | | | | | | | | | | | | | | | | | | | | | | 5 | | | | | |
| | | | | | | | | | | | | | | | | | | | | | | | | | 6 | | | | | |
| | | | | | | | | | | | | | | | | | | | | | | | | | 7 | | | | | |
| | | | | | | | | | | | | | | | | | | | | | | | | | 8 | | | | | |
| | | | | | | | | | | | | | | | | | | | | | | | | | 9 | | | | | |
| | | | | | | | | | | | | | | | | | | | | | | | | | 10 | | | | | |
| | | | | | | | | | | | | | | | | | | | | | | | | | 11 | | | | | |
| | | | | | | | | | | | | | | | | | | | | | | | | | 12 | | | | | |
| | | | | | | | | | | | | | | | | | | | | | | | | | 13 | | | | | |
| | | | | | | | | | | | | | | | | | | | | | | | | | 14 | | | | | |
| | | | | | | | | | | | | | | | | | | | | | | | | | 15 | | | | | |
| | | | | | | | | | | | | | | | | | | | | | | | | | 16 | | | | | |
| | | | | | | | | | | | | | | | | | | | | | | | | | 17 | | | | | |
| | | | | | | | | | | | | | | | | | | | | | | | | | 18 | | | | | |
| | | | | | | | | | | | | | | | | | | | | | | | | | 19 | | | | | |
| | | | | | | | | | | | | | | | | | | | | | | | | | 20 | | | | | |
| | | | | | | | | | | | | | | | | | | | | | | | | | 21 | | | | | |
| | | | | | | | | | | | | | | | | | | | | | | | | | 22 | | | | | |
| | | | | | | | | | | | | | | | | | | | | | | | | | 23 | | | | | |
| | | | | | | | | | | | | | | | | | | | | | | | | | 24 | | | | | |
| | | | | | | | | | | | | | | | | | | | | | | | | | 25 | | | | | |
| | | | | | | | | | | | | | | | | | | | | | | | | | 26 | | | | | |
| | | | | | | | | | | | | | | | | | | | | | | | | | 27 | | | | | |
| | | | | | | | | | | | | | | | | | | | | | | | | | 28 | | | | | |
| | | | | | | | | | | | | | | | | | | | | | | | | | 29 | | | | | |
| | | | | | | | | | | | | | | | | | | | | | | | | | 30 | | | | | |
| | | | | | | | | | | | | | | | | | | | | | | | | | 31 | | | | | |
| | | | | | | | | | | | | | | | | | | | | | | | | | 32 | | | | | |
| | | | | | | | | | | | | | | | | | | | | | | | | | 33 | | | | | |
| | | | | | | | | | | | | | | | | | | | | | | | | | 34 | | | | | |
| | | | | | | | | | | | | | | | | | | | | | | | | | 35 | | | | | |
| | | | | | | | | | | | | | | | | | | | | | | | | | 36 | | | | | |

# $\mathcal{S}$ubject______________________________

| Week | Week____ | | | | | Week____ | | | | | Week____ | | | | | Week____ | | | | | Week____ | | | | | Week____ | | | | |
|---|---|---|---|---|---|---|---|---|---|---|---|---|---|---|---|---|---|---|---|---|---|---|---|---|---|---|
| Day | M | T | W | T | F | M | T | W | T | F | M | T | W | T | F | M | T | W | T | F | M | T | W | T | F |
| Date | | | | | | | | | | | | | | | | | | | | | | | | | |
| *Assignments or Attendance* | | | | | | | | | | | | | | | | | | | | | | | | | |
| Name | | | | | | | | | | | | | | | | | | | | | | | | | |
| 1 | | | | | | | | | | | | | | | | | | | | | | | | | |
| 2 | | | | | | | | | | | | | | | | | | | | | | | | | |
| 3 | | | | | | | | | | | | | | | | | | | | | | | | | |
| 4 | | | | | | | | | | | | | | | | | | | | | | | | | |
| 5 | | | | | | | | | | | | | | | | | | | | | | | | | |
| 6 | | | | | | | | | | | | | | | | | | | | | | | | | |
| 7 | | | | | | | | | | | | | | | | | | | | | | | | | |
| 8 | | | | | | | | | | | | | | | | | | | | | | | | | |
| 9 | | | | | | | | | | | | | | | | | | | | | | | | | |
| 10 | | | | | | | | | | | | | | | | | | | | | | | | | |
| 11 | | | | | | | | | | | | | | | | | | | | | | | | | |
| 12 | | | | | | | | | | | | | | | | | | | | | | | | | |
| 13 | | | | | | | | | | | | | | | | | | | | | | | | | |
| 14 | | | | | | | | | | | | | | | | | | | | | | | | | |
| 15 | | | | | | | | | | | | | | | | | | | | | | | | | |
| 16 | | | | | | | | | | | | | | | | | | | | | | | | | |
| 17 | | | | | | | | | | | | | | | | | | | | | | | | | |
| 18 | | | | | | | | | | | | | | | | | | | | | | | | | |
| 19 | | | | | | | | | | | | | | | | | | | | | | | | | |
| 20 | | | | | | | | | | | | | | | | | | | | | | | | | |
| 21 | | | | | | | | | | | | | | | | | | | | | | | | | |
| 22 | | | | | | | | | | | | | | | | | | | | | | | | | |
| 23 | | | | | | | | | | | | | | | | | | | | | | | | | |
| 24 | | | | | | | | | | | | | | | | | | | | | | | | | |
| 25 | | | | | | | | | | | | | | | | | | | | | | | | | |
| 26 | | | | | | | | | | | | | | | | | | | | | | | | | |
| 27 | | | | | | | | | | | | | | | | | | | | | | | | | |
| 28 | | | | | | | | | | | | | | | | | | | | | | | | | |
| 29 | | | | | | | | | | | | | | | | | | | | | | | | | |
| 30 | | | | | | | | | | | | | | | | | | | | | | | | | |
| 31 | | | | | | | | | | | | | | | | | | | | | | | | | |
| 32 | | | | | | | | | | | | | | | | | | | | | | | | | |
| 33 | | | | | | | | | | | | | | | | | | | | | | | | | |
| 34 | | | | | | | | | | | | | | | | | | | | | | | | | |
| 35 | | | | | | | | | | | | | | | | | | | | | | | | | |
| 36 | | | | | | | | | | | | | | | | | | | | | | | | | |

# *Period*_______________________

| Week____ | | | | | Week____ | | | | | Week____ | | | | | Week____ | | | | | Week____ | | | | | | Days Present | Days Absent | Tardies | Quarter Grade | |
|---|---|---|---|---|---|---|---|---|---|---|---|---|---|---|---|---|---|---|---|---|---|---|---|---|---|---|---|---|---|---|
| M | T | W | T | F | M | T | W | T | F | M | T | W | T | F | M | T | W | T | F | M | T | W | T | F | | | | | | |
| | | | | | | | | | | | | | | | | | | | | | | | | | | | | | | |
| | | | | | | | | | | | | | | | | | | | | | | | | | | | | | | |
| | | | | | | | | | | | | | | | | | | | | | | | | | 1 | | | | | |
| | | | | | | | | | | | | | | | | | | | | | | | | | 2 | | | | | |
| | | | | | | | | | | | | | | | | | | | | | | | | | 3 | | | | | |
| | | | | | | | | | | | | | | | | | | | | | | | | | 4 | | | | | |
| | | | | | | | | | | | | | | | | | | | | | | | | | 5 | | | | | |
| | | | | | | | | | | | | | | | | | | | | | | | | | 6 | | | | | |
| | | | | | | | | | | | | | | | | | | | | | | | | | 7 | | | | | |
| | | | | | | | | | | | | | | | | | | | | | | | | | 8 | | | | | |
| | | | | | | | | | | | | | | | | | | | | | | | | | 9 | | | | | |
| | | | | | | | | | | | | | | | | | | | | | | | | | 10 | | | | | |
| | | | | | | | | | | | | | | | | | | | | | | | | | 11 | | | | | |
| | | | | | | | | | | | | | | | | | | | | | | | | | 12 | | | | | |
| | | | | | | | | | | | | | | | | | | | | | | | | | 13 | | | | | |
| | | | | | | | | | | | | | | | | | | | | | | | | | 14 | | | | | |
| | | | | | | | | | | | | | | | | | | | | | | | | | 15 | | | | | |
| | | | | | | | | | | | | | | | | | | | | | | | | | 16 | | | | | |
| | | | | | | | | | | | | | | | | | | | | | | | | | 17 | | | | | |
| | | | | | | | | | | | | | | | | | | | | | | | | | 18 | | | | | |
| | | | | | | | | | | | | | | | | | | | | | | | | | 19 | | | | | |
| | | | | | | | | | | | | | | | | | | | | | | | | | 20 | | | | | |
| | | | | | | | | | | | | | | | | | | | | | | | | | 21 | | | | | |
| | | | | | | | | | | | | | | | | | | | | | | | | | 22 | | | | | |
| | | | | | | | | | | | | | | | | | | | | | | | | | 23 | | | | | |
| | | | | | | | | | | | | | | | | | | | | | | | | | 24 | | | | | |
| | | | | | | | | | | | | | | | | | | | | | | | | | 25 | | | | | |
| | | | | | | | | | | | | | | | | | | | | | | | | | 26 | | | | | |
| | | | | | | | | | | | | | | | | | | | | | | | | | 27 | | | | | |
| | | | | | | | | | | | | | | | | | | | | | | | | | 28 | | | | | |
| | | | | | | | | | | | | | | | | | | | | | | | | | 29 | | | | | |
| | | | | | | | | | | | | | | | | | | | | | | | | | 30 | | | | | |
| | | | | | | | | | | | | | | | | | | | | | | | | | 31 | | | | | |
| | | | | | | | | | | | | | | | | | | | | | | | | | 32 | | | | | |
| | | | | | | | | | | | | | | | | | | | | | | | | | 33 | | | | | |
| | | | | | | | | | | | | | | | | | | | | | | | | | 34 | | | | | |
| | | | | | | | | | | | | | | | | | | | | | | | | | 35 | | | | | |
| | | | | | | | | | | | | | | | | | | | | | | | | | 36 | | | | | |

# $\mathcal{S}$ubject________________________

| Week | Week____ | | | | | Week____ | | | | | Week____ | | | | | Week____ | | | | | Week____ | | | | | Week____ | | | | |
|---|---|---|---|---|---|---|---|---|---|---|---|---|---|---|---|---|---|---|---|---|---|---|---|---|---|
| Day | M | T | W | T | F | M | T | W | T | F | M | T | W | T | F | M | T | W | T | F | M | T | W | T | F |
| Date | | | | | | | | | | | | | | | | | | | | | | | | | |
| Assignments or Attendance | | | | | | | | | | | | | | | | | | | | | | | | | |
| Name | | | | | | | | | | | | | | | | | | | | | | | | | |
| 1 | | | | | | | | | | | | | | | | | | | | | | | | | |
| 2 | | | | | | | | | | | | | | | | | | | | | | | | | |
| 3 | | | | | | | | | | | | | | | | | | | | | | | | | |
| 4 | | | | | | | | | | | | | | | | | | | | | | | | | |
| 5 | | | | | | | | | | | | | | | | | | | | | | | | | |
| 6 | | | | | | | | | | | | | | | | | | | | | | | | | |
| 7 | | | | | | | | | | | | | | | | | | | | | | | | | |
| 8 | | | | | | | | | | | | | | | | | | | | | | | | | |
| 9 | | | | | | | | | | | | | | | | | | | | | | | | | |
| 10 | | | | | | | | | | | | | | | | | | | | | | | | | |
| 11 | | | | | | | | | | | | | | | | | | | | | | | | | |
| 12 | | | | | | | | | | | | | | | | | | | | | | | | | |
| 13 | | | | | | | | | | | | | | | | | | | | | | | | | |
| 14 | | | | | | | | | | | | | | | | | | | | | | | | | |
| 15 | | | | | | | | | | | | | | | | | | | | | | | | | |
| 16 | | | | | | | | | | | | | | | | | | | | | | | | | |
| 17 | | | | | | | | | | | | | | | | | | | | | | | | | |
| 18 | | | | | | | | | | | | | | | | | | | | | | | | | |
| 19 | | | | | | | | | | | | | | | | | | | | | | | | | |
| 20 | | | | | | | | | | | | | | | | | | | | | | | | | |
| 21 | | | | | | | | | | | | | | | | | | | | | | | | | |
| 22 | | | | | | | | | | | | | | | | | | | | | | | | | |
| 23 | | | | | | | | | | | | | | | | | | | | | | | | | |
| 24 | | | | | | | | | | | | | | | | | | | | | | | | | |
| 25 | | | | | | | | | | | | | | | | | | | | | | | | | |
| 26 | | | | | | | | | | | | | | | | | | | | | | | | | |
| 27 | | | | | | | | | | | | | | | | | | | | | | | | | |
| 28 | | | | | | | | | | | | | | | | | | | | | | | | | |
| 29 | | | | | | | | | | | | | | | | | | | | | | | | | |
| 30 | | | | | | | | | | | | | | | | | | | | | | | | | |
| 31 | | | | | | | | | | | | | | | | | | | | | | | | | |
| 32 | | | | | | | | | | | | | | | | | | | | | | | | | |
| 33 | | | | | | | | | | | | | | | | | | | | | | | | | |
| 34 | | | | | | | | | | | | | | | | | | | | | | | | | |
| 35 | | | | | | | | | | | | | | | | | | | | | | | | | |
| 36 | | | | | | | | | | | | | | | | | | | | | | | | | |

# *Period*________________________

| Week____ | | | | | Week____ | | | | | Week____ | | | | | Week____ | | | | | Week____ | | | | | *Days Present* | *Days Absent* | *Tardies* | *Quarter Grade* | |
|---|---|---|---|---|---|---|---|---|---|---|---|---|---|---|---|---|---|---|---|---|---|---|---|---|---|---|---|---|---|
| M | T | W | T | F | M | T | W | T | F | M | T | W | T | F | M | T | W | T | F | M | T | W | T | F | | | | | |
| | | | | | | | | | | | | | | | | | | | | | | | | | 1 | | | | |
| | | | | | | | | | | | | | | | | | | | | | | | | | 2 | | | | |
| | | | | | | | | | | | | | | | | | | | | | | | | | 3 | | | | |
| | | | | | | | | | | | | | | | | | | | | | | | | | 4 | | | | |
| | | | | | | | | | | | | | | | | | | | | | | | | | 5 | | | | |
| | | | | | | | | | | | | | | | | | | | | | | | | | 6 | | | | |
| | | | | | | | | | | | | | | | | | | | | | | | | | 7 | | | | |
| | | | | | | | | | | | | | | | | | | | | | | | | | 8 | | | | |
| | | | | | | | | | | | | | | | | | | | | | | | | | 9 | | | | |
| | | | | | | | | | | | | | | | | | | | | | | | | | 10 | | | | |
| | | | | | | | | | | | | | | | | | | | | | | | | | 11 | | | | |
| | | | | | | | | | | | | | | | | | | | | | | | | | 12 | | | | |
| | | | | | | | | | | | | | | | | | | | | | | | | | 13 | | | | |
| | | | | | | | | | | | | | | | | | | | | | | | | | 14 | | | | |
| | | | | | | | | | | | | | | | | | | | | | | | | | 15 | | | | |
| | | | | | | | | | | | | | | | | | | | | | | | | | 16 | | | | |
| | | | | | | | | | | | | | | | | | | | | | | | | | 17 | | | | |
| | | | | | | | | | | | | | | | | | | | | | | | | | 18 | | | | |
| | | | | | | | | | | | | | | | | | | | | | | | | | 19 | | | | |
| | | | | | | | | | | | | | | | | | | | | | | | | | 20 | | | | |
| | | | | | | | | | | | | | | | | | | | | | | | | | 21 | | | | |
| | | | | | | | | | | | | | | | | | | | | | | | | | 22 | | | | |
| | | | | | | | | | | | | | | | | | | | | | | | | | 23 | | | | |
| | | | | | | | | | | | | | | | | | | | | | | | | | 24 | | | | |
| | | | | | | | | | | | | | | | | | | | | | | | | | 25 | | | | |
| | | | | | | | | | | | | | | | | | | | | | | | | | 26 | | | | |
| | | | | | | | | | | | | | | | | | | | | | | | | | 27 | | | | |
| | | | | | | | | | | | | | | | | | | | | | | | | | 28 | | | | |
| | | | | | | | | | | | | | | | | | | | | | | | | | 29 | | | | |
| | | | | | | | | | | | | | | | | | | | | | | | | | 30 | | | | |
| | | | | | | | | | | | | | | | | | | | | | | | | | 31 | | | | |
| | | | | | | | | | | | | | | | | | | | | | | | | | 32 | | | | |
| | | | | | | | | | | | | | | | | | | | | | | | | | 33 | | | | |
| | | | | | | | | | | | | | | | | | | | | | | | | | 34 | | | | |
| | | | | | | | | | | | | | | | | | | | | | | | | | 35 | | | | |
| | | | | | | | | | | | | | | | | | | | | | | | | | 36 | | | | |

# $\mathcal{S}$ubject________________________

| Week | Week____ | | | | | Week____ | | | | | Week____ | | | | | Week____ | | | | | Week____ | | | | |
|---|---|---|---|---|---|---|---|---|---|---|---|---|---|---|---|---|---|---|---|---|---|---|---|---|---|
| **Day** | M | T | W | T | F | M | T | W | T | F | M | T | W | T | F | M | T | W | T | F | M | T | W | T | F |
| **Date** | | | | | | | | | | | | | | | | | | | | | | | | | |
| *Assignments or Attendance* | | | | | | | | | | | | | | | | | | | | | | | | | |
| *Name* | | | | | | | | | | | | | | | | | | | | | | | | | |
| 1 | | | | | | | | | | | | | | | | | | | | | | | | | |
| 2 | | | | | | | | | | | | | | | | | | | | | | | | | |
| 3 | | | | | | | | | | | | | | | | | | | | | | | | | |
| 4 | | | | | | | | | | | | | | | | | | | | | | | | | |
| 5 | | | | | | | | | | | | | | | | | | | | | | | | | |
| 6 | | | | | | | | | | | | | | | | | | | | | | | | | |
| 7 | | | | | | | | | | | | | | | | | | | | | | | | | |
| 8 | | | | | | | | | | | | | | | | | | | | | | | | | |
| 9 | | | | | | | | | | | | | | | | | | | | | | | | | |
| 10 | | | | | | | | | | | | | | | | | | | | | | | | | |
| 11 | | | | | | | | | | | | | | | | | | | | | | | | | |
| 12 | | | | | | | | | | | | | | | | | | | | | | | | | |
| 13 | | | | | | | | | | | | | | | | | | | | | | | | | |
| 14 | | | | | | | | | | | | | | | | | | | | | | | | | |
| 15 | | | | | | | | | | | | | | | | | | | | | | | | | |
| 16 | | | | | | | | | | | | | | | | | | | | | | | | | |
| 17 | | | | | | | | | | | | | | | | | | | | | | | | | |
| 18 | | | | | | | | | | | | | | | | | | | | | | | | | |
| 19 | | | | | | | | | | | | | | | | | | | | | | | | | |
| 20 | | | | | | | | | | | | | | | | | | | | | | | | | |
| 21 | | | | | | | | | | | | | | | | | | | | | | | | | |
| 22 | | | | | | | | | | | | | | | | | | | | | | | | | |
| 23 | | | | | | | | | | | | | | | | | | | | | | | | | |
| 24 | | | | | | | | | | | | | | | | | | | | | | | | | |
| 25 | | | | | | | | | | | | | | | | | | | | | | | | | |
| 26 | | | | | | | | | | | | | | | | | | | | | | | | | |
| 27 | | | | | | | | | | | | | | | | | | | | | | | | | |
| 28 | | | | | | | | | | | | | | | | | | | | | | | | | |
| 29 | | | | | | | | | | | | | | | | | | | | | | | | | |
| 30 | | | | | | | | | | | | | | | | | | | | | | | | | |
| 31 | | | | | | | | | | | | | | | | | | | | | | | | | |
| 32 | | | | | | | | | | | | | | | | | | | | | | | | | |
| 33 | | | | | | | | | | | | | | | | | | | | | | | | | |
| 34 | | | | | | | | | | | | | | | | | | | | | | | | | |
| 35 | | | | | | | | | | | | | | | | | | | | | | | | | |
| 36 | | | | | | | | | | | | | | | | | | | | | | | | | |

# *Period*__________________

| | Week____ | | | | Week____ | | | | Week____ | | | | Week____ | | | | Week____ | | | | | Days Present | Days Absent | Tardies | Quarter Grade | |
|---|---|---|---|---|---|---|---|---|---|---|---|---|---|---|---|---|---|---|---|---|---|---|---|---|---|---|
| M | T | W | T | F | M | T | W | T | F | M | T | W | T | F | M | T | W | T | F | M | T | W | T | F | | | | | |
| | | | | | | | | | | | | | | | | | | | | | | | | | 1 | | | | |
| | | | | | | | | | | | | | | | | | | | | | | | | | 2 | | | | |
| | | | | | | | | | | | | | | | | | | | | | | | | | 3 | | | | |
| | | | | | | | | | | | | | | | | | | | | | | | | | 4 | | | | |
| | | | | | | | | | | | | | | | | | | | | | | | | | 5 | | | | |
| | | | | | | | | | | | | | | | | | | | | | | | | | 6 | | | | |
| | | | | | | | | | | | | | | | | | | | | | | | | | 7 | | | | |
| | | | | | | | | | | | | | | | | | | | | | | | | | 8 | | | | |
| | | | | | | | | | | | | | | | | | | | | | | | | | 9 | | | | |
| | | | | | | | | | | | | | | | | | | | | | | | | | 10 | | | | |
| | | | | | | | | | | | | | | | | | | | | | | | | | 11 | | | | |
| | | | | | | | | | | | | | | | | | | | | | | | | | 12 | | | | |
| | | | | | | | | | | | | | | | | | | | | | | | | | 13 | | | | |
| | | | | | | | | | | | | | | | | | | | | | | | | | 14 | | | | |
| | | | | | | | | | | | | | | | | | | | | | | | | | 15 | | | | |
| | | | | | | | | | | | | | | | | | | | | | | | | | 16 | | | | |
| | | | | | | | | | | | | | | | | | | | | | | | | | 17 | | | | |
| | | | | | | | | | | | | | | | | | | | | | | | | | 18 | | | | |
| | | | | | | | | | | | | | | | | | | | | | | | | | 19 | | | | |
| | | | | | | | | | | | | | | | | | | | | | | | | | 20 | | | | |
| | | | | | | | | | | | | | | | | | | | | | | | | | 21 | | | | |
| | | | | | | | | | | | | | | | | | | | | | | | | | 22 | | | | |
| | | | | | | | | | | | | | | | | | | | | | | | | | 23 | | | | |
| | | | | | | | | | | | | | | | | | | | | | | | | | 24 | | | | |
| | | | | | | | | | | | | | | | | | | | | | | | | | 25 | | | | |
| | | | | | | | | | | | | | | | | | | | | | | | | | 26 | | | | |
| | | | | | | | | | | | | | | | | | | | | | | | | | 27 | | | | |
| | | | | | | | | | | | | | | | | | | | | | | | | | 28 | | | | |
| | | | | | | | | | | | | | | | | | | | | | | | | | 29 | | | | |
| | | | | | | | | | | | | | | | | | | | | | | | | | 30 | | | | |
| | | | | | | | | | | | | | | | | | | | | | | | | | 31 | | | | |
| | | | | | | | | | | | | | | | | | | | | | | | | | 32 | | | | |
| | | | | | | | | | | | | | | | | | | | | | | | | | 33 | | | | |
| | | | | | | | | | | | | | | | | | | | | | | | | | 34 | | | | |
| | | | | | | | | | | | | | | | | | | | | | | | | | 35 | | | | |
| | | | | | | | | | | | | | | | | | | | | | | | | | 36 | | | | |

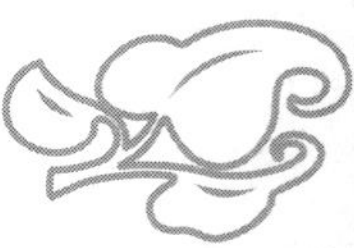

# Subject________________________

| Week | Week____ | | | | | Week____ | | | | | Week____ | | | | | Week____ | | | | | Week____ | | | | | Week____ | | | | |
|---|---|---|---|---|---|---|---|---|---|---|---|---|---|---|---|---|---|---|---|---|---|---|---|---|---|
| Day | M | T | W | T | F | M | T | W | T | F | M | T | W | T | F | M | T | W | T | F | M | T | W | T | F |
| Date | | | | | | | | | | | | | | | | | | | | | | | | | |
| Assignments or Attendance | | | | | | | | | | | | | | | | | | | | | | | | | |
| Name | | | | | | | | | | | | | | | | | | | | | | | | | |
| 1 | | | | | | | | | | | | | | | | | | | | | | | | | |
| 2 | | | | | | | | | | | | | | | | | | | | | | | | | |
| 3 | | | | | | | | | | | | | | | | | | | | | | | | | |
| 4 | | | | | | | | | | | | | | | | | | | | | | | | | |
| 5 | | | | | | | | | | | | | | | | | | | | | | | | | |
| 6 | | | | | | | | | | | | | | | | | | | | | | | | | |
| 7 | | | | | | | | | | | | | | | | | | | | | | | | | |
| 8 | | | | | | | | | | | | | | | | | | | | | | | | | |
| 9 | | | | | | | | | | | | | | | | | | | | | | | | | |
| 10 | | | | | | | | | | | | | | | | | | | | | | | | | |
| 11 | | | | | | | | | | | | | | | | | | | | | | | | | |
| 12 | | | | | | | | | | | | | | | | | | | | | | | | | |
| 13 | | | | | | | | | | | | | | | | | | | | | | | | | |
| 14 | | | | | | | | | | | | | | | | | | | | | | | | | |
| 15 | | | | | | | | | | | | | | | | | | | | | | | | | |
| 16 | | | | | | | | | | | | | | | | | | | | | | | | | |
| 17 | | | | | | | | | | | | | | | | | | | | | | | | | |
| 18 | | | | | | | | | | | | | | | | | | | | | | | | | |
| 19 | | | | | | | | | | | | | | | | | | | | | | | | | |
| 20 | | | | | | | | | | | | | | | | | | | | | | | | | |
| 21 | | | | | | | | | | | | | | | | | | | | | | | | | |
| 22 | | | | | | | | | | | | | | | | | | | | | | | | | |
| 23 | | | | | | | | | | | | | | | | | | | | | | | | | |
| 24 | | | | | | | | | | | | | | | | | | | | | | | | | |
| 25 | | | | | | | | | | | | | | | | | | | | | | | | | |
| 26 | | | | | | | | | | | | | | | | | | | | | | | | | |
| 27 | | | | | | | | | | | | | | | | | | | | | | | | | |
| 28 | | | | | | | | | | | | | | | | | | | | | | | | | |
| 29 | | | | | | | | | | | | | | | | | | | | | | | | | |
| 30 | | | | | | | | | | | | | | | | | | | | | | | | | |
| 31 | | | | | | | | | | | | | | | | | | | | | | | | | |
| 32 | | | | | | | | | | | | | | | | | | | | | | | | | |
| 33 | | | | | | | | | | | | | | | | | | | | | | | | | |
| 34 | | | | | | | | | | | | | | | | | | | | | | | | | |
| 35 | | | | | | | | | | | | | | | | | | | | | | | | | |
| 36 | | | | | | | | | | | | | | | | | | | | | | | | | |

# _Period_____________________

| Week____ | | | | | Week____ | | | | | Week____ | | | | | Week____ | | | | | Week____ | | | | | | Days Present | Days Absent | Tardies | Quarter Grade | |
|---|---|---|---|---|---|---|---|---|---|---|---|---|---|---|---|---|---|---|---|---|---|---|---|---|---|---|---|---|---|---|
| M | T | W | T | F | M | T | W | T | F | M | T | W | T | F | M | T | W | T | F | M | T | W | T | F | | | | | | |
| | | | | | | | | | | | | | | | | | | | | | | | | | 1 | | | | | |
| | | | | | | | | | | | | | | | | | | | | | | | | | 2 | | | | | |
| | | | | | | | | | | | | | | | | | | | | | | | | | 3 | | | | | |
| | | | | | | | | | | | | | | | | | | | | | | | | | 4 | | | | | |
| | | | | | | | | | | | | | | | | | | | | | | | | | 5 | | | | | |
| | | | | | | | | | | | | | | | | | | | | | | | | | 6 | | | | | |
| | | | | | | | | | | | | | | | | | | | | | | | | | 7 | | | | | |
| | | | | | | | | | | | | | | | | | | | | | | | | | 8 | | | | | |
| | | | | | | | | | | | | | | | | | | | | | | | | | 9 | | | | | |
| | | | | | | | | | | | | | | | | | | | | | | | | | 10 | | | | | |
| | | | | | | | | | | | | | | | | | | | | | | | | | 11 | | | | | |
| | | | | | | | | | | | | | | | | | | | | | | | | | 12 | | | | | |
| | | | | | | | | | | | | | | | | | | | | | | | | | 13 | | | | | |
| | | | | | | | | | | | | | | | | | | | | | | | | | 14 | | | | | |
| | | | | | | | | | | | | | | | | | | | | | | | | | 15 | | | | | |
| | | | | | | | | | | | | | | | | | | | | | | | | | 16 | | | | | |
| | | | | | | | | | | | | | | | | | | | | | | | | | 17 | | | | | |
| | | | | | | | | | | | | | | | | | | | | | | | | | 18 | | | | | |
| | | | | | | | | | | | | | | | | | | | | | | | | | 19 | | | | | |
| | | | | | | | | | | | | | | | | | | | | | | | | | 20 | | | | | |
| | | | | | | | | | | | | | | | | | | | | | | | | | 21 | | | | | |
| | | | | | | | | | | | | | | | | | | | | | | | | | 22 | | | | | |
| | | | | | | | | | | | | | | | | | | | | | | | | | 23 | | | | | |
| | | | | | | | | | | | | | | | | | | | | | | | | | 24 | | | | | |
| | | | | | | | | | | | | | | | | | | | | | | | | | 25 | | | | | |
| | | | | | | | | | | | | | | | | | | | | | | | | | 26 | | | | | |
| | | | | | | | | | | | | | | | | | | | | | | | | | 27 | | | | | |
| | | | | | | | | | | | | | | | | | | | | | | | | | 28 | | | | | |
| | | | | | | | | | | | | | | | | | | | | | | | | | 29 | | | | | |
| | | | | | | | | | | | | | | | | | | | | | | | | | 30 | | | | | |
| | | | | | | | | | | | | | | | | | | | | | | | | | 31 | | | | | |
| | | | | | | | | | | | | | | | | | | | | | | | | | 32 | | | | | |
| | | | | | | | | | | | | | | | | | | | | | | | | | 33 | | | | | |
| | | | | | | | | | | | | | | | | | | | | | | | | | 34 | | | | | |
| | | | | | | | | | | | | | | | | | | | | | | | | | 35 | | | | | |
| | | | | | | | | | | | | | | | | | | | | | | | | | 36 | | | | | |

# Subject_______________________

| Week | Week____ | | | | | Week____ | | | | | Week____ | | | | | Week____ | | | | | Week____ | | | | | Week____ | | | |
|---|---|---|---|---|---|---|---|---|---|---|---|---|---|---|---|---|---|---|---|---|---|---|---|---|---|---|---|---|---|
| Day | M | T | W | T | F | M | T | W | T | F | M | T | W | T | F | M | T | W | T | F | M | T | W | T | F | M | T | W | T | F |
| Date | | | | | | | | | | | | | | | | | | | | | | | | | | | | | | |
| Assignments or Attendance | | | | | | | | | | | | | | | | | | | | | | | | | | | | | | |
| Name | | | | | | | | | | | | | | | | | | | | | | | | | | | | | | |
| 1 | | | | | | | | | | | | | | | | | | | | | | | | | | | | | | |
| 2 | | | | | | | | | | | | | | | | | | | | | | | | | | | | | | |
| 3 | | | | | | | | | | | | | | | | | | | | | | | | | | | | | | |
| 4 | | | | | | | | | | | | | | | | | | | | | | | | | | | | | | |
| 5 | | | | | | | | | | | | | | | | | | | | | | | | | | | | | | |
| 6 | | | | | | | | | | | | | | | | | | | | | | | | | | | | | | |
| 7 | | | | | | | | | | | | | | | | | | | | | | | | | | | | | | |
| 8 | | | | | | | | | | | | | | | | | | | | | | | | | | | | | | |
| 9 | | | | | | | | | | | | | | | | | | | | | | | | | | | | | | |
| 10 | | | | | | | | | | | | | | | | | | | | | | | | | | | | | | |
| 11 | | | | | | | | | | | | | | | | | | | | | | | | | | | | | | |
| 12 | | | | | | | | | | | | | | | | | | | | | | | | | | | | | | |
| 13 | | | | | | | | | | | | | | | | | | | | | | | | | | | | | | |
| 14 | | | | | | | | | | | | | | | | | | | | | | | | | | | | | | |
| 15 | | | | | | | | | | | | | | | | | | | | | | | | | | | | | | |
| 16 | | | | | | | | | | | | | | | | | | | | | | | | | | | | | | |
| 17 | | | | | | | | | | | | | | | | | | | | | | | | | | | | | | |
| 18 | | | | | | | | | | | | | | | | | | | | | | | | | | | | | | |
| 19 | | | | | | | | | | | | | | | | | | | | | | | | | | | | | | |
| 20 | | | | | | | | | | | | | | | | | | | | | | | | | | | | | | |
| 21 | | | | | | | | | | | | | | | | | | | | | | | | | | | | | | |
| 22 | | | | | | | | | | | | | | | | | | | | | | | | | | | | | | |
| 23 | | | | | | | | | | | | | | | | | | | | | | | | | | | | | | |
| 24 | | | | | | | | | | | | | | | | | | | | | | | | | | | | | | |
| 25 | | | | | | | | | | | | | | | | | | | | | | | | | | | | | | |
| 26 | | | | | | | | | | | | | | | | | | | | | | | | | | | | | | |
| 27 | | | | | | | | | | | | | | | | | | | | | | | | | | | | | | |
| 28 | | | | | | | | | | | | | | | | | | | | | | | | | | | | | | |
| 29 | | | | | | | | | | | | | | | | | | | | | | | | | | | | | | |
| 30 | | | | | | | | | | | | | | | | | | | | | | | | | | | | | | |
| 31 | | | | | | | | | | | | | | | | | | | | | | | | | | | | | | |
| 32 | | | | | | | | | | | | | | | | | | | | | | | | | | | | | | |
| 33 | | | | | | | | | | | | | | | | | | | | | | | | | | | | | | |
| 34 | | | | | | | | | | | | | | | | | | | | | | | | | | | | | | |
| 35 | | | | | | | | | | | | | | | | | | | | | | | | | | | | | | |
| 36 | | | | | | | | | | | | | | | | | | | | | | | | | | | | | | |

# *Period*_______________________

| Week____ | | | | | Week____ | | | | | Week____ | | | | | Week____ | | | | | Week____ | | | | | | Days Present | Days Absent | Tardies | Quarter Grade | |
|---|---|---|---|---|---|---|---|---|---|---|---|---|---|---|---|---|---|---|---|---|---|---|---|---|---|---|---|---|---|---|
| M | T | W | T | F | M | T | W | T | F | M | T | W | T | F | M | T | W | T | F | M | T | W | T | F | | | | | | |
| | | | | | | | | | | | | | | | | | | | | | | | | | | | | | | |
| | | | | | | | | | | | | | | | | | | | | | | | | | 1 | | | | | |
| | | | | | | | | | | | | | | | | | | | | | | | | | 2 | | | | | |
| | | | | | | | | | | | | | | | | | | | | | | | | | 3 | | | | | |
| | | | | | | | | | | | | | | | | | | | | | | | | | 4 | | | | | |
| | | | | | | | | | | | | | | | | | | | | | | | | | 5 | | | | | |
| | | | | | | | | | | | | | | | | | | | | | | | | | 6 | | | | | |
| | | | | | | | | | | | | | | | | | | | | | | | | | 7 | | | | | |
| | | | | | | | | | | | | | | | | | | | | | | | | | 8 | | | | | |
| | | | | | | | | | | | | | | | | | | | | | | | | | 9 | | | | | |
| | | | | | | | | | | | | | | | | | | | | | | | | | 10 | | | | | |
| | | | | | | | | | | | | | | | | | | | | | | | | | 11 | | | | | |
| | | | | | | | | | | | | | | | | | | | | | | | | | 12 | | | | | |
| | | | | | | | | | | | | | | | | | | | | | | | | | 13 | | | | | |
| | | | | | | | | | | | | | | | | | | | | | | | | | 14 | | | | | |
| | | | | | | | | | | | | | | | | | | | | | | | | | 15 | | | | | |
| | | | | | | | | | | | | | | | | | | | | | | | | | 16 | | | | | |
| | | | | | | | | | | | | | | | | | | | | | | | | | 17 | | | | | |
| | | | | | | | | | | | | | | | | | | | | | | | | | 18 | | | | | |
| | | | | | | | | | | | | | | | | | | | | | | | | | 19 | | | | | |
| | | | | | | | | | | | | | | | | | | | | | | | | | 20 | | | | | |
| | | | | | | | | | | | | | | | | | | | | | | | | | 21 | | | | | |
| | | | | | | | | | | | | | | | | | | | | | | | | | 22 | | | | | |
| | | | | | | | | | | | | | | | | | | | | | | | | | 23 | | | | | |
| | | | | | | | | | | | | | | | | | | | | | | | | | 24 | | | | | |
| | | | | | | | | | | | | | | | | | | | | | | | | | 25 | | | | | |
| | | | | | | | | | | | | | | | | | | | | | | | | | 26 | | | | | |
| | | | | | | | | | | | | | | | | | | | | | | | | | 27 | | | | | |
| | | | | | | | | | | | | | | | | | | | | | | | | | 28 | | | | | |
| | | | | | | | | | | | | | | | | | | | | | | | | | 29 | | | | | |
| | | | | | | | | | | | | | | | | | | | | | | | | | 30 | | | | | |
| | | | | | | | | | | | | | | | | | | | | | | | | | 31 | | | | | |
| | | | | | | | | | | | | | | | | | | | | | | | | | 32 | | | | | |
| | | | | | | | | | | | | | | | | | | | | | | | | | 33 | | | | | |
| | | | | | | | | | | | | | | | | | | | | | | | | | 34 | | | | | |
| | | | | | | | | | | | | | | | | | | | | | | | | | 35 | | | | | |
| | | | | | | | | | | | | | | | | | | | | | | | | | 36 | | | | | |

# $\mathcal{S}$ubject________________________

| Week | Week____ | | | | | Week____ | | | | | Week____ | | | | | Week____ | | | | | Week____ | | | | | Week____ | | | | |
|---|---|---|---|---|---|---|---|---|---|---|---|---|---|---|---|---|---|---|---|---|---|---|---|---|---|---|
| Day | M | T | W | T | F | M | T | W | T | F | M | T | W | T | F | M | T | W | T | F | M | T | W | T | F | M | T | W | T | F |
| Date | | | | | | | | | | | | | | | | | | | | | | | | | |
| Assignments or Attendance | | | | | | | | | | | | | | | | | | | | | | | | | |
| Name | | | | | | | | | | | | | | | | | | | | | | | | | |
| 1 | | | | | | | | | | | | | | | | | | | | | | | | | |
| 2 | | | | | | | | | | | | | | | | | | | | | | | | | |
| 3 | | | | | | | | | | | | | | | | | | | | | | | | | |
| 4 | | | | | | | | | | | | | | | | | | | | | | | | | |
| 5 | | | | | | | | | | | | | | | | | | | | | | | | | |
| 6 | | | | | | | | | | | | | | | | | | | | | | | | | |
| 7 | | | | | | | | | | | | | | | | | | | | | | | | | |
| 8 | | | | | | | | | | | | | | | | | | | | | | | | | |
| 9 | | | | | | | | | | | | | | | | | | | | | | | | | |
| 10 | | | | | | | | | | | | | | | | | | | | | | | | | |
| 11 | | | | | | | | | | | | | | | | | | | | | | | | | |
| 12 | | | | | | | | | | | | | | | | | | | | | | | | | |
| 13 | | | | | | | | | | | | | | | | | | | | | | | | | |
| 14 | | | | | | | | | | | | | | | | | | | | | | | | | |
| 15 | | | | | | | | | | | | | | | | | | | | | | | | | |
| 16 | | | | | | | | | | | | | | | | | | | | | | | | | |
| 17 | | | | | | | | | | | | | | | | | | | | | | | | | |
| 18 | | | | | | | | | | | | | | | | | | | | | | | | | |
| 19 | | | | | | | | | | | | | | | | | | | | | | | | | |
| 20 | | | | | | | | | | | | | | | | | | | | | | | | | |
| 21 | | | | | | | | | | | | | | | | | | | | | | | | | |
| 22 | | | | | | | | | | | | | | | | | | | | | | | | | |
| 23 | | | | | | | | | | | | | | | | | | | | | | | | | |
| 24 | | | | | | | | | | | | | | | | | | | | | | | | | |
| 25 | | | | | | | | | | | | | | | | | | | | | | | | | |
| 26 | | | | | | | | | | | | | | | | | | | | | | | | | |
| 27 | | | | | | | | | | | | | | | | | | | | | | | | | |
| 28 | | | | | | | | | | | | | | | | | | | | | | | | | |
| 29 | | | | | | | | | | | | | | | | | | | | | | | | | |
| 30 | | | | | | | | | | | | | | | | | | | | | | | | | |
| 31 | | | | | | | | | | | | | | | | | | | | | | | | | |
| 32 | | | | | | | | | | | | | | | | | | | | | | | | | |
| 33 | | | | | | | | | | | | | | | | | | | | | | | | | |
| 34 | | | | | | | | | | | | | | | | | | | | | | | | | |
| 35 | | | | | | | | | | | | | | | | | | | | | | | | | |
| 36 | | | | | | | | | | | | | | | | | | | | | | | | | |

# Period__________________________

| Week____ | | | | | Week____ | | | | | Week____ | | | | | Week____ | | | | | Week____ | | | | | | Days Present | Days Absent | Tardies | Quarter Grade | |
|---|---|---|---|---|---|---|---|---|---|---|---|---|---|---|---|---|---|---|---|---|---|---|---|---|---|---|---|---|---|---|
| M | T | W | T | F | M | T | W | T | F | M | T | W | T | F | M | T | W | T | F | M | T | W | T | F | | | | | | |
| | | | | | | | | | | | | | | | | | | | | | | | | | 1 | | | | | |
| | | | | | | | | | | | | | | | | | | | | | | | | | 2 | | | | | |
| | | | | | | | | | | | | | | | | | | | | | | | | | 3 | | | | | |
| | | | | | | | | | | | | | | | | | | | | | | | | | 4 | | | | | |
| | | | | | | | | | | | | | | | | | | | | | | | | | 5 | | | | | |
| | | | | | | | | | | | | | | | | | | | | | | | | | 6 | | | | | |
| | | | | | | | | | | | | | | | | | | | | | | | | | 7 | | | | | |
| | | | | | | | | | | | | | | | | | | | | | | | | | 8 | | | | | |
| | | | | | | | | | | | | | | | | | | | | | | | | | 9 | | | | | |
| | | | | | | | | | | | | | | | | | | | | | | | | | 10 | | | | | |
| | | | | | | | | | | | | | | | | | | | | | | | | | 11 | | | | | |
| | | | | | | | | | | | | | | | | | | | | | | | | | 12 | | | | | |
| | | | | | | | | | | | | | | | | | | | | | | | | | 13 | | | | | |
| | | | | | | | | | | | | | | | | | | | | | | | | | 14 | | | | | |
| | | | | | | | | | | | | | | | | | | | | | | | | | 15 | | | | | |
| | | | | | | | | | | | | | | | | | | | | | | | | | 16 | | | | | |
| | | | | | | | | | | | | | | | | | | | | | | | | | 17 | | | | | |
| | | | | | | | | | | | | | | | | | | | | | | | | | 18 | | | | | |
| | | | | | | | | | | | | | | | | | | | | | | | | | 19 | | | | | |
| | | | | | | | | | | | | | | | | | | | | | | | | | 20 | | | | | |
| | | | | | | | | | | | | | | | | | | | | | | | | | 21 | | | | | |
| | | | | | | | | | | | | | | | | | | | | | | | | | 22 | | | | | |
| | | | | | | | | | | | | | | | | | | | | | | | | | 23 | | | | | |
| | | | | | | | | | | | | | | | | | | | | | | | | | 24 | | | | | |
| | | | | | | | | | | | | | | | | | | | | | | | | | 25 | | | | | |
| | | | | | | | | | | | | | | | | | | | | | | | | | 26 | | | | | |
| | | | | | | | | | | | | | | | | | | | | | | | | | 27 | | | | | |
| | | | | | | | | | | | | | | | | | | | | | | | | | 28 | | | | | |
| | | | | | | | | | | | | | | | | | | | | | | | | | 29 | | | | | |
| | | | | | | | | | | | | | | | | | | | | | | | | | 30 | | | | | |
| | | | | | | | | | | | | | | | | | | | | | | | | | 31 | | | | | |
| | | | | | | | | | | | | | | | | | | | | | | | | | 32 | | | | | |
| | | | | | | | | | | | | | | | | | | | | | | | | | 33 | | | | | |
| | | | | | | | | | | | | | | | | | | | | | | | | | 34 | | | | | |
| | | | | | | | | | | | | | | | | | | | | | | | | | 35 | | | | | |
| | | | | | | | | | | | | | | | | | | | | | | | | | 36 | | | | | |

# $\mathscr{S}$ubject______________________________

| Week | Week____ | | | | | Week____ | | | | | Week____ | | | | | Week____ | | | | | Week____ | | | | | Week____ | | | | |
|---|---|---|---|---|---|---|---|---|---|---|---|---|---|---|---|---|---|---|---|---|---|---|---|---|---|
| Day | M | T | W | T | F | M | T | W | T | F | M | T | W | T | F | M | T | W | T | F | M | T | W | T | F |
| Date | | | | | | | | | | | | | | | | | | | | | | | | | |
| Assignments or Attendance | | | | | | | | | | | | | | | | | | | | | | | | | |
| Name | | | | | | | | | | | | | | | | | | | | | | | | | |
| 1 | | | | | | | | | | | | | | | | | | | | | | | | | |
| 2 | | | | | | | | | | | | | | | | | | | | | | | | | |
| 3 | | | | | | | | | | | | | | | | | | | | | | | | | |
| 4 | | | | | | | | | | | | | | | | | | | | | | | | | |
| 5 | | | | | | | | | | | | | | | | | | | | | | | | | |
| 6 | | | | | | | | | | | | | | | | | | | | | | | | | |
| 7 | | | | | | | | | | | | | | | | | | | | | | | | | |
| 8 | | | | | | | | | | | | | | | | | | | | | | | | | |
| 9 | | | | | | | | | | | | | | | | | | | | | | | | | |
| 10 | | | | | | | | | | | | | | | | | | | | | | | | | |
| 11 | | | | | | | | | | | | | | | | | | | | | | | | | |
| 12 | | | | | | | | | | | | | | | | | | | | | | | | | |
| 13 | | | | | | | | | | | | | | | | | | | | | | | | | |
| 14 | | | | | | | | | | | | | | | | | | | | | | | | | |
| 15 | | | | | | | | | | | | | | | | | | | | | | | | | |
| 16 | | | | | | | | | | | | | | | | | | | | | | | | | |
| 17 | | | | | | | | | | | | | | | | | | | | | | | | | |
| 18 | | | | | | | | | | | | | | | | | | | | | | | | | |
| 19 | | | | | | | | | | | | | | | | | | | | | | | | | |
| 20 | | | | | | | | | | | | | | | | | | | | | | | | | |
| 21 | | | | | | | | | | | | | | | | | | | | | | | | | |
| 22 | | | | | | | | | | | | | | | | | | | | | | | | | |
| 23 | | | | | | | | | | | | | | | | | | | | | | | | | |
| 24 | | | | | | | | | | | | | | | | | | | | | | | | | |
| 25 | | | | | | | | | | | | | | | | | | | | | | | | | |
| 26 | | | | | | | | | | | | | | | | | | | | | | | | | |
| 27 | | | | | | | | | | | | | | | | | | | | | | | | | |
| 28 | | | | | | | | | | | | | | | | | | | | | | | | | |
| 29 | | | | | | | | | | | | | | | | | | | | | | | | | |
| 30 | | | | | | | | | | | | | | | | | | | | | | | | | |
| 31 | | | | | | | | | | | | | | | | | | | | | | | | | |
| 32 | | | | | | | | | | | | | | | | | | | | | | | | | |
| 33 | | | | | | | | | | | | | | | | | | | | | | | | | |
| 34 | | | | | | | | | | | | | | | | | | | | | | | | | |
| 35 | | | | | | | | | | | | | | | | | | | | | | | | | |
| 36 | | | | | | | | | | | | | | | | | | | | | | | | | |

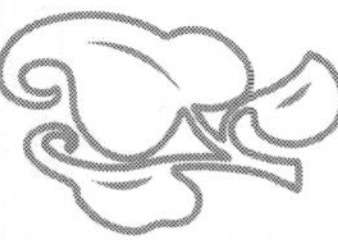

# *Period*______________________

| | | | | | | | | | | | | | | | | | | | | | | | | | | Days Present | Days Absent | Tardies | Quarter Grade | |
|---|---|---|---|---|---|---|---|---|---|---|---|---|---|---|---|---|---|---|---|---|---|---|---|---|---|---|---|---|---|---|---|
| *Week*____ | | | | | *Week*____ | | | | | *Week*____ | | | | | *Week*____ | | | | | *Week*____ | | | | | | | | | | |
| M | T | W | T | F | M | T | W | T | F | M | T | W | T | F | M | T | W | T | F | M | T | W | T | F | | | | | | |
| | | | | | | | | | | | | | | | | | | | | | | | | | | | | | | |
| | | | | | | | | | | | | | | | | | | | | | | | | | 1 | | | | | |
| | | | | | | | | | | | | | | | | | | | | | | | | | 2 | | | | | |
| | | | | | | | | | | | | | | | | | | | | | | | | | 3 | | | | | |
| | | | | | | | | | | | | | | | | | | | | | | | | | 4 | | | | | |
| | | | | | | | | | | | | | | | | | | | | | | | | | 5 | | | | | |
| | | | | | | | | | | | | | | | | | | | | | | | | | 6 | | | | | |
| | | | | | | | | | | | | | | | | | | | | | | | | | 7 | | | | | |
| | | | | | | | | | | | | | | | | | | | | | | | | | 8 | | | | | |
| | | | | | | | | | | | | | | | | | | | | | | | | | 9 | | | | | |
| | | | | | | | | | | | | | | | | | | | | | | | | | 10 | | | | | |
| | | | | | | | | | | | | | | | | | | | | | | | | | 11 | | | | | |
| | | | | | | | | | | | | | | | | | | | | | | | | | 12 | | | | | |
| | | | | | | | | | | | | | | | | | | | | | | | | | 13 | | | | | |
| | | | | | | | | | | | | | | | | | | | | | | | | | 14 | | | | | |
| | | | | | | | | | | | | | | | | | | | | | | | | | 15 | | | | | |
| | | | | | | | | | | | | | | | | | | | | | | | | | 16 | | | | | |
| | | | | | | | | | | | | | | | | | | | | | | | | | 17 | | | | | |
| | | | | | | | | | | | | | | | | | | | | | | | | | 18 | | | | | |
| | | | | | | | | | | | | | | | | | | | | | | | | | 19 | | | | | |
| | | | | | | | | | | | | | | | | | | | | | | | | | 20 | | | | | |
| | | | | | | | | | | | | | | | | | | | | | | | | | 21 | | | | | |
| | | | | | | | | | | | | | | | | | | | | | | | | | 22 | | | | | |
| | | | | | | | | | | | | | | | | | | | | | | | | | 23 | | | | | |
| | | | | | | | | | | | | | | | | | | | | | | | | | 24 | | | | | |
| | | | | | | | | | | | | | | | | | | | | | | | | | 25 | | | | | |
| | | | | | | | | | | | | | | | | | | | | | | | | | 26 | | | | | |
| | | | | | | | | | | | | | | | | | | | | | | | | | 27 | | | | | |
| | | | | | | | | | | | | | | | | | | | | | | | | | 28 | | | | | |
| | | | | | | | | | | | | | | | | | | | | | | | | | 29 | | | | | |
| | | | | | | | | | | | | | | | | | | | | | | | | | 30 | | | | | |
| | | | | | | | | | | | | | | | | | | | | | | | | | 31 | | | | | |
| | | | | | | | | | | | | | | | | | | | | | | | | | 32 | | | | | |
| | | | | | | | | | | | | | | | | | | | | | | | | | 33 | | | | | |
| | | | | | | | | | | | | | | | | | | | | | | | | | 34 | | | | | |
| | | | | | | | | | | | | | | | | | | | | | | | | | 35 | | | | | |
| | | | | | | | | | | | | | | | | | | | | | | | | | 36 | | | | | |

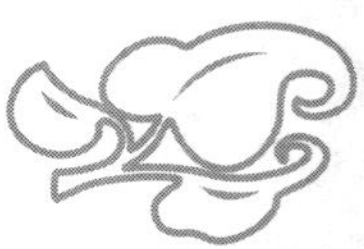

# $\mathcal{S}$ubject _______________________

| Week | Week____ | | | | | Week____ | | | | | Week____ | | | | | Week____ | | | | | Week____ | | | | | Week____ | | | | |
|---|---|---|---|---|---|---|---|---|---|---|---|---|---|---|---|---|---|---|---|---|---|---|---|---|---|---|
| Day | M | T | W | T | F | M | T | W | T | F | M | T | W | T | F | M | T | W | T | F | M | T | W | T | F |
| Date | | | | | | | | | | | | | | | | | | | | | | | | | |
| Assignments or Attendance | | | | | | | | | | | | | | | | | | | | | | | | | |
| Name | | | | | | | | | | | | | | | | | | | | | | | | | |
| 1 | | | | | | | | | | | | | | | | | | | | | | | | | |
| 2 | | | | | | | | | | | | | | | | | | | | | | | | | |
| 3 | | | | | | | | | | | | | | | | | | | | | | | | | |
| 4 | | | | | | | | | | | | | | | | | | | | | | | | | |
| 5 | | | | | | | | | | | | | | | | | | | | | | | | | |
| 6 | | | | | | | | | | | | | | | | | | | | | | | | | |
| 7 | | | | | | | | | | | | | | | | | | | | | | | | | |
| 8 | | | | | | | | | | | | | | | | | | | | | | | | | |
| 9 | | | | | | | | | | | | | | | | | | | | | | | | | |
| 10 | | | | | | | | | | | | | | | | | | | | | | | | | |
| 11 | | | | | | | | | | | | | | | | | | | | | | | | | |
| 12 | | | | | | | | | | | | | | | | | | | | | | | | | |
| 13 | | | | | | | | | | | | | | | | | | | | | | | | | |
| 14 | | | | | | | | | | | | | | | | | | | | | | | | | |
| 15 | | | | | | | | | | | | | | | | | | | | | | | | | |
| 16 | | | | | | | | | | | | | | | | | | | | | | | | | |
| 17 | | | | | | | | | | | | | | | | | | | | | | | | | |
| 18 | | | | | | | | | | | | | | | | | | | | | | | | | |
| 19 | | | | | | | | | | | | | | | | | | | | | | | | | |
| 20 | | | | | | | | | | | | | | | | | | | | | | | | | |
| 21 | | | | | | | | | | | | | | | | | | | | | | | | | |
| 22 | | | | | | | | | | | | | | | | | | | | | | | | | |
| 23 | | | | | | | | | | | | | | | | | | | | | | | | | |
| 24 | | | | | | | | | | | | | | | | | | | | | | | | | |
| 25 | | | | | | | | | | | | | | | | | | | | | | | | | |
| 26 | | | | | | | | | | | | | | | | | | | | | | | | | |
| 27 | | | | | | | | | | | | | | | | | | | | | | | | | |
| 28 | | | | | | | | | | | | | | | | | | | | | | | | | |
| 29 | | | | | | | | | | | | | | | | | | | | | | | | | |
| 30 | | | | | | | | | | | | | | | | | | | | | | | | | |
| 31 | | | | | | | | | | | | | | | | | | | | | | | | | |
| 32 | | | | | | | | | | | | | | | | | | | | | | | | | |
| 33 | | | | | | | | | | | | | | | | | | | | | | | | | |
| 34 | | | | | | | | | | | | | | | | | | | | | | | | | |
| 35 | | | | | | | | | | | | | | | | | | | | | | | | | |
| 36 | | | | | | | | | | | | | | | | | | | | | | | | | |

# *Period*____________________

| Week____ | | | | | Week____ | | | | | Week____ | | | | | Week____ | | | | | Week____ | | | | | | Days Present | Days Absent | Tardies | Quarter Grade | |
|---|---|---|---|---|---|---|---|---|---|---|---|---|---|---|---|---|---|---|---|---|---|---|---|---|---|---|---|---|---|---|
| M | T | W | T | F | M | T | W | T | F | M | T | W | T | F | M | T | W | T | F | M | T | W | T | F | 1 | | | | | |
| | | | | | | | | | | | | | | | | | | | | | | | | | 2 | | | | | |
| | | | | | | | | | | | | | | | | | | | | | | | | | 3 | | | | | |
| | | | | | | | | | | | | | | | | | | | | | | | | | 4 | | | | | |
| | | | | | | | | | | | | | | | | | | | | | | | | | 5 | | | | | |
| | | | | | | | | | | | | | | | | | | | | | | | | | 6 | | | | | |
| | | | | | | | | | | | | | | | | | | | | | | | | | 7 | | | | | |
| | | | | | | | | | | | | | | | | | | | | | | | | | 8 | | | | | |
| | | | | | | | | | | | | | | | | | | | | | | | | | 9 | | | | | |
| | | | | | | | | | | | | | | | | | | | | | | | | | 10 | | | | | |
| | | | | | | | | | | | | | | | | | | | | | | | | | 11 | | | | | |
| | | | | | | | | | | | | | | | | | | | | | | | | | 12 | | | | | |
| | | | | | | | | | | | | | | | | | | | | | | | | | 13 | | | | | |
| | | | | | | | | | | | | | | | | | | | | | | | | | 14 | | | | | |
| | | | | | | | | | | | | | | | | | | | | | | | | | 15 | | | | | |
| | | | | | | | | | | | | | | | | | | | | | | | | | 16 | | | | | |
| | | | | | | | | | | | | | | | | | | | | | | | | | 17 | | | | | |
| | | | | | | | | | | | | | | | | | | | | | | | | | 18 | | | | | |
| | | | | | | | | | | | | | | | | | | | | | | | | | 19 | | | | | |
| | | | | | | | | | | | | | | | | | | | | | | | | | 20 | | | | | |
| | | | | | | | | | | | | | | | | | | | | | | | | | 21 | | | | | |
| | | | | | | | | | | | | | | | | | | | | | | | | | 22 | | | | | |
| | | | | | | | | | | | | | | | | | | | | | | | | | 23 | | | | | |
| | | | | | | | | | | | | | | | | | | | | | | | | | 24 | | | | | |
| | | | | | | | | | | | | | | | | | | | | | | | | | 25 | | | | | |
| | | | | | | | | | | | | | | | | | | | | | | | | | 26 | | | | | |
| | | | | | | | | | | | | | | | | | | | | | | | | | 27 | | | | | |
| | | | | | | | | | | | | | | | | | | | | | | | | | 28 | | | | | |
| | | | | | | | | | | | | | | | | | | | | | | | | | 29 | | | | | |
| | | | | | | | | | | | | | | | | | | | | | | | | | 30 | | | | | |
| | | | | | | | | | | | | | | | | | | | | | | | | | 31 | | | | | |
| | | | | | | | | | | | | | | | | | | | | | | | | | 32 | | | | | |
| | | | | | | | | | | | | | | | | | | | | | | | | | 33 | | | | | |
| | | | | | | | | | | | | | | | | | | | | | | | | | 34 | | | | | |
| | | | | | | | | | | | | | | | | | | | | | | | | | 35 | | | | | |
| | | | | | | | | | | | | | | | | | | | | | | | | | 36 | | | | | |

# $\mathcal{S}$ubject________________________

| Week | Week____ | | | | | Week____ | | | | | Week____ | | | | | Week____ | | | | | Week____ | | | | |
|---|---|---|---|---|---|---|---|---|---|---|---|---|---|---|---|---|---|---|---|---|---|---|---|---|---|
| Day | M | T | W | T | F | M | T | W | T | F | M | T | W | T | F | M | T | W | T | F | M | T | W | T | F |
| Date | | | | | | | | | | | | | | | | | | | | | | | | | |
| Assignments or Attendance | | | | | | | | | | | | | | | | | | | | | | | | | |
| Name | | | | | | | | | | | | | | | | | | | | | | | | | |
| 1 | | | | | | | | | | | | | | | | | | | | | | | | | |
| 2 | | | | | | | | | | | | | | | | | | | | | | | | | |
| 3 | | | | | | | | | | | | | | | | | | | | | | | | | |
| 4 | | | | | | | | | | | | | | | | | | | | | | | | | |
| 5 | | | | | | | | | | | | | | | | | | | | | | | | | |
| 6 | | | | | | | | | | | | | | | | | | | | | | | | | |
| 7 | | | | | | | | | | | | | | | | | | | | | | | | | |
| 8 | | | | | | | | | | | | | | | | | | | | | | | | | |
| 9 | | | | | | | | | | | | | | | | | | | | | | | | | |
| 10 | | | | | | | | | | | | | | | | | | | | | | | | | |
| 11 | | | | | | | | | | | | | | | | | | | | | | | | | |
| 12 | | | | | | | | | | | | | | | | | | | | | | | | | |
| 13 | | | | | | | | | | | | | | | | | | | | | | | | | |
| 14 | | | | | | | | | | | | | | | | | | | | | | | | | |
| 15 | | | | | | | | | | | | | | | | | | | | | | | | | |
| 16 | | | | | | | | | | | | | | | | | | | | | | | | | |
| 17 | | | | | | | | | | | | | | | | | | | | | | | | | |
| 18 | | | | | | | | | | | | | | | | | | | | | | | | | |
| 19 | | | | | | | | | | | | | | | | | | | | | | | | | |
| 20 | | | | | | | | | | | | | | | | | | | | | | | | | |
| 21 | | | | | | | | | | | | | | | | | | | | | | | | | |
| 22 | | | | | | | | | | | | | | | | | | | | | | | | | |
| 23 | | | | | | | | | | | | | | | | | | | | | | | | | |
| 24 | | | | | | | | | | | | | | | | | | | | | | | | | |
| 25 | | | | | | | | | | | | | | | | | | | | | | | | | |
| 26 | | | | | | | | | | | | | | | | | | | | | | | | | |
| 27 | | | | | | | | | | | | | | | | | | | | | | | | | |
| 28 | | | | | | | | | | | | | | | | | | | | | | | | | |
| 29 | | | | | | | | | | | | | | | | | | | | | | | | | |
| 30 | | | | | | | | | | | | | | | | | | | | | | | | | |
| 31 | | | | | | | | | | | | | | | | | | | | | | | | | |
| 32 | | | | | | | | | | | | | | | | | | | | | | | | | |
| 33 | | | | | | | | | | | | | | | | | | | | | | | | | |
| 34 | | | | | | | | | | | | | | | | | | | | | | | | | |
| 35 | | | | | | | | | | | | | | | | | | | | | | | | | |
| 36 | | | | | | | | | | | | | | | | | | | | | | | | | |

# *Period*___________________

| Week____ | | | | | Week____ | | | | | Week____ | | | | | Week____ | | | | | Week____ | | | | | | Days Present | Days Absent | Tardies | Quarter Grade | |
|---|---|---|---|---|---|---|---|---|---|---|---|---|---|---|---|---|---|---|---|---|---|---|---|---|---|---|---|---|---|---|
| M | T | W | T | F | M | T | W | T | F | M | T | W | T | F | M | T | W | T | F | M | T | W | T | F | | | | | | |
| | | | | | | | | | | | | | | | | | | | | | | | | | | | | | | |
| | | | | | | | | | | | | | | | | | | | | | | | | | 1 | | | | | |
| | | | | | | | | | | | | | | | | | | | | | | | | | 2 | | | | | |
| | | | | | | | | | | | | | | | | | | | | | | | | | 3 | | | | | |
| | | | | | | | | | | | | | | | | | | | | | | | | | 4 | | | | | |
| | | | | | | | | | | | | | | | | | | | | | | | | | 5 | | | | | |
| | | | | | | | | | | | | | | | | | | | | | | | | | 6 | | | | | |
| | | | | | | | | | | | | | | | | | | | | | | | | | 7 | | | | | |
| | | | | | | | | | | | | | | | | | | | | | | | | | 8 | | | | | |
| | | | | | | | | | | | | | | | | | | | | | | | | | 9 | | | | | |
| | | | | | | | | | | | | | | | | | | | | | | | | | 10 | | | | | |
| | | | | | | | | | | | | | | | | | | | | | | | | | 11 | | | | | |
| | | | | | | | | | | | | | | | | | | | | | | | | | 12 | | | | | |
| | | | | | | | | | | | | | | | | | | | | | | | | | 13 | | | | | |
| | | | | | | | | | | | | | | | | | | | | | | | | | 14 | | | | | |
| | | | | | | | | | | | | | | | | | | | | | | | | | 15 | | | | | |
| | | | | | | | | | | | | | | | | | | | | | | | | | 16 | | | | | |
| | | | | | | | | | | | | | | | | | | | | | | | | | 17 | | | | | |
| | | | | | | | | | | | | | | | | | | | | | | | | | 18 | | | | | |
| | | | | | | | | | | | | | | | | | | | | | | | | | 19 | | | | | |
| | | | | | | | | | | | | | | | | | | | | | | | | | 20 | | | | | |
| | | | | | | | | | | | | | | | | | | | | | | | | | 21 | | | | | |
| | | | | | | | | | | | | | | | | | | | | | | | | | 22 | | | | | |
| | | | | | | | | | | | | | | | | | | | | | | | | | 23 | | | | | |
| | | | | | | | | | | | | | | | | | | | | | | | | | 24 | | | | | |
| | | | | | | | | | | | | | | | | | | | | | | | | | 25 | | | | | |
| | | | | | | | | | | | | | | | | | | | | | | | | | 26 | | | | | |
| | | | | | | | | | | | | | | | | | | | | | | | | | 27 | | | | | |
| | | | | | | | | | | | | | | | | | | | | | | | | | 28 | | | | | |
| | | | | | | | | | | | | | | | | | | | | | | | | | 29 | | | | | |
| | | | | | | | | | | | | | | | | | | | | | | | | | 30 | | | | | |
| | | | | | | | | | | | | | | | | | | | | | | | | | 31 | | | | | |
| | | | | | | | | | | | | | | | | | | | | | | | | | 32 | | | | | |
| | | | | | | | | | | | | | | | | | | | | | | | | | 33 | | | | | |
| | | | | | | | | | | | | | | | | | | | | | | | | | 34 | | | | | |
| | | | | | | | | | | | | | | | | | | | | | | | | | 35 | | | | | |
| | | | | | | | | | | | | | | | | | | | | | | | | | 36 | | | | | |

# $S$ubject_______________________

| Week | Week____ | | | | | Week____ | | | | | Week____ | | | | | Week____ | | | | | Week____ | | | | |
|---|---|---|---|---|---|---|---|---|---|---|---|---|---|---|---|---|---|---|---|---|---|---|---|---|---|
| Day | M | T | W | T | F | M | T | W | T | F | M | T | W | T | F | M | T | W | T | F | M | T | W | T | F |
| Date | | | | | | | | | | | | | | | | | | | | | | | | | |
| Assignments or Attendance | | | | | | | | | | | | | | | | | | | | | | | | | |
| Name | | | | | | | | | | | | | | | | | | | | | | | | | |
| 1 | | | | | | | | | | | | | | | | | | | | | | | | | |
| 2 | | | | | | | | | | | | | | | | | | | | | | | | | |
| 3 | | | | | | | | | | | | | | | | | | | | | | | | | |
| 4 | | | | | | | | | | | | | | | | | | | | | | | | | |
| 5 | | | | | | | | | | | | | | | | | | | | | | | | | |
| 6 | | | | | | | | | | | | | | | | | | | | | | | | | |
| 7 | | | | | | | | | | | | | | | | | | | | | | | | | |
| 8 | | | | | | | | | | | | | | | | | | | | | | | | | |
| 9 | | | | | | | | | | | | | | | | | | | | | | | | | |
| 10 | | | | | | | | | | | | | | | | | | | | | | | | | |
| 11 | | | | | | | | | | | | | | | | | | | | | | | | | |
| 12 | | | | | | | | | | | | | | | | | | | | | | | | | |
| 13 | | | | | | | | | | | | | | | | | | | | | | | | | |
| 14 | | | | | | | | | | | | | | | | | | | | | | | | | |
| 15 | | | | | | | | | | | | | | | | | | | | | | | | | |
| 16 | | | | | | | | | | | | | | | | | | | | | | | | | |
| 17 | | | | | | | | | | | | | | | | | | | | | | | | | |
| 18 | | | | | | | | | | | | | | | | | | | | | | | | | |
| 19 | | | | | | | | | | | | | | | | | | | | | | | | | |
| 20 | | | | | | | | | | | | | | | | | | | | | | | | | |
| 21 | | | | | | | | | | | | | | | | | | | | | | | | | |
| 22 | | | | | | | | | | | | | | | | | | | | | | | | | |
| 23 | | | | | | | | | | | | | | | | | | | | | | | | | |
| 24 | | | | | | | | | | | | | | | | | | | | | | | | | |
| 25 | | | | | | | | | | | | | | | | | | | | | | | | | |
| 26 | | | | | | | | | | | | | | | | | | | | | | | | | |
| 27 | | | | | | | | | | | | | | | | | | | | | | | | | |
| 28 | | | | | | | | | | | | | | | | | | | | | | | | | |
| 29 | | | | | | | | | | | | | | | | | | | | | | | | | |
| 30 | | | | | | | | | | | | | | | | | | | | | | | | | |
| 31 | | | | | | | | | | | | | | | | | | | | | | | | | |
| 32 | | | | | | | | | | | | | | | | | | | | | | | | | |
| 33 | | | | | | | | | | | | | | | | | | | | | | | | | |
| 34 | | | | | | | | | | | | | | | | | | | | | | | | | |
| 35 | | | | | | | | | | | | | | | | | | | | | | | | | |
| 36 | | | | | | | | | | | | | | | | | | | | | | | | | |

# *Period* _______________________

| Week____ | | | | | Week____ | | | | | Week____ | | | | | Week____ | | | | | Week____ | | | | | | Days Present | Days Absent | Tardies | Quarter Grade | | |
|---|---|---|---|---|---|---|---|---|---|---|---|---|---|---|---|---|---|---|---|---|---|---|---|---|---|---|---|---|---|
| M | T | W | T | F | M | T | W | T | F | M | T | W | T | F | M | T | W | T | F | M | T | W | T | F | | | | | | | |
| | | | | | | | | | | | | | | | | | | | | | | | | | | | | | | | |
| | | | | | | | | | | | | | | | | | | | | | | | | | | | | | | | |
| | | | | | | | | | | | | | | | | | | | | | | | | | 1 | | | | | | |
| | | | | | | | | | | | | | | | | | | | | | | | | | 2 | | | | | | |
| | | | | | | | | | | | | | | | | | | | | | | | | | 3 | | | | | | |
| | | | | | | | | | | | | | | | | | | | | | | | | | 4 | | | | | | |
| | | | | | | | | | | | | | | | | | | | | | | | | | 5 | | | | | | |
| | | | | | | | | | | | | | | | | | | | | | | | | | 6 | | | | | | |
| | | | | | | | | | | | | | | | | | | | | | | | | | 7 | | | | | | |
| | | | | | | | | | | | | | | | | | | | | | | | | | 8 | | | | | | |
| | | | | | | | | | | | | | | | | | | | | | | | | | 9 | | | | | | |
| | | | | | | | | | | | | | | | | | | | | | | | | | 10 | | | | | | |
| | | | | | | | | | | | | | | | | | | | | | | | | | 11 | | | | | | |
| | | | | | | | | | | | | | | | | | | | | | | | | | 12 | | | | | | |
| | | | | | | | | | | | | | | | | | | | | | | | | | 13 | | | | | | |
| | | | | | | | | | | | | | | | | | | | | | | | | | 14 | | | | | | |
| | | | | | | | | | | | | | | | | | | | | | | | | | 15 | | | | | | |
| | | | | | | | | | | | | | | | | | | | | | | | | | 16 | | | | | | |
| | | | | | | | | | | | | | | | | | | | | | | | | | 17 | | | | | | |
| | | | | | | | | | | | | | | | | | | | | | | | | | 18 | | | | | | |
| | | | | | | | | | | | | | | | | | | | | | | | | | 19 | | | | | | |
| | | | | | | | | | | | | | | | | | | | | | | | | | 20 | | | | | | |
| | | | | | | | | | | | | | | | | | | | | | | | | | 21 | | | | | | |
| | | | | | | | | | | | | | | | | | | | | | | | | | 22 | | | | | | |
| | | | | | | | | | | | | | | | | | | | | | | | | | 23 | | | | | | |
| | | | | | | | | | | | | | | | | | | | | | | | | | 24 | | | | | | |
| | | | | | | | | | | | | | | | | | | | | | | | | | 25 | | | | | | |
| | | | | | | | | | | | | | | | | | | | | | | | | | 26 | | | | | | |
| | | | | | | | | | | | | | | | | | | | | | | | | | 27 | | | | | | |
| | | | | | | | | | | | | | | | | | | | | | | | | | 28 | | | | | | |
| | | | | | | | | | | | | | | | | | | | | | | | | | 29 | | | | | | |
| | | | | | | | | | | | | | | | | | | | | | | | | | 30 | | | | | | |
| | | | | | | | | | | | | | | | | | | | | | | | | | 31 | | | | | | |
| | | | | | | | | | | | | | | | | | | | | | | | | | 32 | | | | | | |
| | | | | | | | | | | | | | | | | | | | | | | | | | 33 | | | | | | |
| | | | | | | | | | | | | | | | | | | | | | | | | | 34 | | | | | | |
| | | | | | | | | | | | | | | | | | | | | | | | | | 35 | | | | | | |
| | | | | | | | | | | | | | | | | | | | | | | | | | 36 | | | | | | |

# $\mathcal{S}$ubject______________________

| Week | Week____ | | | | | Week____ | | | | | Week____ | | | | | Week____ | | | | | Week____ | | | | | Week____ | | | | |
|---|---|---|---|---|---|---|---|---|---|---|---|---|---|---|---|---|---|---|---|---|---|---|---|---|---|
| Day | M | T | W | T | F | M | T | W | T | F | M | T | W | T | F | M | T | W | T | F | M | T | W | T | F |
| Date | | | | | | | | | | | | | | | | | | | | | | | | | |
| Assignments or Attendance | | | | | | | | | | | | | | | | | | | | | | | | | |
| Name | | | | | | | | | | | | | | | | | | | | | | | | | |
| 1 | | | | | | | | | | | | | | | | | | | | | | | | | |
| 2 | | | | | | | | | | | | | | | | | | | | | | | | | |
| 3 | | | | | | | | | | | | | | | | | | | | | | | | | |
| 4 | | | | | | | | | | | | | | | | | | | | | | | | | |
| 5 | | | | | | | | | | | | | | | | | | | | | | | | | |
| 6 | | | | | | | | | | | | | | | | | | | | | | | | | |
| 7 | | | | | | | | | | | | | | | | | | | | | | | | | |
| 8 | | | | | | | | | | | | | | | | | | | | | | | | | |
| 9 | | | | | | | | | | | | | | | | | | | | | | | | | |
| 10 | | | | | | | | | | | | | | | | | | | | | | | | | |
| 11 | | | | | | | | | | | | | | | | | | | | | | | | | |
| 12 | | | | | | | | | | | | | | | | | | | | | | | | | |
| 13 | | | | | | | | | | | | | | | | | | | | | | | | | |
| 14 | | | | | | | | | | | | | | | | | | | | | | | | | |
| 15 | | | | | | | | | | | | | | | | | | | | | | | | | |
| 16 | | | | | | | | | | | | | | | | | | | | | | | | | |
| 17 | | | | | | | | | | | | | | | | | | | | | | | | | |
| 18 | | | | | | | | | | | | | | | | | | | | | | | | | |
| 19 | | | | | | | | | | | | | | | | | | | | | | | | | |
| 20 | | | | | | | | | | | | | | | | | | | | | | | | | |
| 21 | | | | | | | | | | | | | | | | | | | | | | | | | |
| 22 | | | | | | | | | | | | | | | | | | | | | | | | | |
| 23 | | | | | | | | | | | | | | | | | | | | | | | | | |
| 24 | | | | | | | | | | | | | | | | | | | | | | | | | |
| 25 | | | | | | | | | | | | | | | | | | | | | | | | | |
| 26 | | | | | | | | | | | | | | | | | | | | | | | | | |
| 27 | | | | | | | | | | | | | | | | | | | | | | | | | |
| 28 | | | | | | | | | | | | | | | | | | | | | | | | | |
| 29 | | | | | | | | | | | | | | | | | | | | | | | | | |
| 30 | | | | | | | | | | | | | | | | | | | | | | | | | |
| 31 | | | | | | | | | | | | | | | | | | | | | | | | | |
| 32 | | | | | | | | | | | | | | | | | | | | | | | | | |
| 33 | | | | | | | | | | | | | | | | | | | | | | | | | |
| 34 | | | | | | | | | | | | | | | | | | | | | | | | | |
| 35 | | | | | | | | | | | | | | | | | | | | | | | | | |
| 36 | | | | | | | | | | | | | | | | | | | | | | | | | |

# $\mathcal{P}$eriod_____________________

| Week____ | | | | | Week____ | | | | | Week____ | | | | | Week____ | | | | | Week____ | | | | | | Days Present | Days Absent | Tardies | Quarter Grade | | |
|---|---|---|---|---|---|---|---|---|---|---|---|---|---|---|---|---|---|---|---|---|---|---|---|---|---|---|---|---|---|---|---|
| M | T | W | T | F | M | T | W | T | F | M | T | W | T | F | M | T | W | T | F | M | T | W | T | F | | | | | | | |
| | | | | | | | | | | | | | | | | | | | | | | | | | | | | | | | |
| | | | | | | | | | | | | | | | | | | | | | | | | | | | | | | | |
| | | | | | | | | | | | | | | | | | | | | | | | | | 1 | | | | | | |
| | | | | | | | | | | | | | | | | | | | | | | | | | 2 | | | | | | |
| | | | | | | | | | | | | | | | | | | | | | | | | | 3 | | | | | | |
| | | | | | | | | | | | | | | | | | | | | | | | | | 4 | | | | | | |
| | | | | | | | | | | | | | | | | | | | | | | | | | 5 | | | | | | |
| | | | | | | | | | | | | | | | | | | | | | | | | | 6 | | | | | | |
| | | | | | | | | | | | | | | | | | | | | | | | | | 7 | | | | | | |
| | | | | | | | | | | | | | | | | | | | | | | | | | 8 | | | | | | |
| | | | | | | | | | | | | | | | | | | | | | | | | | 9 | | | | | | |
| | | | | | | | | | | | | | | | | | | | | | | | | | 10 | | | | | | |
| | | | | | | | | | | | | | | | | | | | | | | | | | 11 | | | | | | |
| | | | | | | | | | | | | | | | | | | | | | | | | | 12 | | | | | | |
| | | | | | | | | | | | | | | | | | | | | | | | | | 13 | | | | | | |
| | | | | | | | | | | | | | | | | | | | | | | | | | 14 | | | | | | |
| | | | | | | | | | | | | | | | | | | | | | | | | | 15 | | | | | | |
| | | | | | | | | | | | | | | | | | | | | | | | | | 16 | | | | | | |
| | | | | | | | | | | | | | | | | | | | | | | | | | 17 | | | | | | |
| | | | | | | | | | | | | | | | | | | | | | | | | | 18 | | | | | | |
| | | | | | | | | | | | | | | | | | | | | | | | | | 19 | | | | | | |
| | | | | | | | | | | | | | | | | | | | | | | | | | 20 | | | | | | |
| | | | | | | | | | | | | | | | | | | | | | | | | | 21 | | | | | | |
| | | | | | | | | | | | | | | | | | | | | | | | | | 22 | | | | | | |
| | | | | | | | | | | | | | | | | | | | | | | | | | 23 | | | | | | |
| | | | | | | | | | | | | | | | | | | | | | | | | | 24 | | | | | | |
| | | | | | | | | | | | | | | | | | | | | | | | | | 25 | | | | | | |
| | | | | | | | | | | | | | | | | | | | | | | | | | 26 | | | | | | |
| | | | | | | | | | | | | | | | | | | | | | | | | | 27 | | | | | | |
| | | | | | | | | | | | | | | | | | | | | | | | | | 28 | | | | | | |
| | | | | | | | | | | | | | | | | | | | | | | | | | 29 | | | | | | |
| | | | | | | | | | | | | | | | | | | | | | | | | | 30 | | | | | | |
| | | | | | | | | | | | | | | | | | | | | | | | | | 31 | | | | | | |
| | | | | | | | | | | | | | | | | | | | | | | | | | 32 | | | | | | |
| | | | | | | | | | | | | | | | | | | | | | | | | | 33 | | | | | | |
| | | | | | | | | | | | | | | | | | | | | | | | | | 34 | | | | | | |
| | | | | | | | | | | | | | | | | | | | | | | | | | 35 | | | | | | |
| | | | | | | | | | | | | | | | | | | | | | | | | | 36 | | | | | | |

# $\mathscr{S}$ubject______________________________

| Week | Week____ | | | | | Week____ | | | | | Week____ | | | | | Week____ | | | | | Week____ | | | | | Week____ | | | | |
|---|---|---|---|---|---|---|---|---|---|---|---|---|---|---|---|---|---|---|---|---|---|---|---|---|---|---|---|---|---|---|
| Day | M | T | W | T | F | M | T | W | T | F | M | T | W | T | F | M | T | W | T | F | M | T | W | T | F | M | T | W | T | F |
| Date | | | | | | | | | | | | | | | | | | | | | | | | | | | | | | |
| Assignments or Attendance | | | | | | | | | | | | | | | | | | | | | | | | | | | | | | |
| Name | | | | | | | | | | | | | | | | | | | | | | | | | | | | | | |
| 1 | | | | | | | | | | | | | | | | | | | | | | | | | | | | | | |
| 2 | | | | | | | | | | | | | | | | | | | | | | | | | | | | | | |
| 3 | | | | | | | | | | | | | | | | | | | | | | | | | | | | | | |
| 4 | | | | | | | | | | | | | | | | | | | | | | | | | | | | | | |
| 5 | | | | | | | | | | | | | | | | | | | | | | | | | | | | | | |
| 6 | | | | | | | | | | | | | | | | | | | | | | | | | | | | | | |
| 7 | | | | | | | | | | | | | | | | | | | | | | | | | | | | | | |
| 8 | | | | | | | | | | | | | | | | | | | | | | | | | | | | | | |
| 9 | | | | | | | | | | | | | | | | | | | | | | | | | | | | | | |
| 10 | | | | | | | | | | | | | | | | | | | | | | | | | | | | | | |
| 11 | | | | | | | | | | | | | | | | | | | | | | | | | | | | | | |
| 12 | | | | | | | | | | | | | | | | | | | | | | | | | | | | | | |
| 13 | | | | | | | | | | | | | | | | | | | | | | | | | | | | | | |
| 14 | | | | | | | | | | | | | | | | | | | | | | | | | | | | | | |
| 15 | | | | | | | | | | | | | | | | | | | | | | | | | | | | | | |
| 16 | | | | | | | | | | | | | | | | | | | | | | | | | | | | | | |
| 17 | | | | | | | | | | | | | | | | | | | | | | | | | | | | | | |
| 18 | | | | | | | | | | | | | | | | | | | | | | | | | | | | | | |
| 19 | | | | | | | | | | | | | | | | | | | | | | | | | | | | | | |
| 20 | | | | | | | | | | | | | | | | | | | | | | | | | | | | | | |
| 21 | | | | | | | | | | | | | | | | | | | | | | | | | | | | | | |
| 22 | | | | | | | | | | | | | | | | | | | | | | | | | | | | | | |
| 23 | | | | | | | | | | | | | | | | | | | | | | | | | | | | | | |
| 24 | | | | | | | | | | | | | | | | | | | | | | | | | | | | | | |
| 25 | | | | | | | | | | | | | | | | | | | | | | | | | | | | | | |
| 26 | | | | | | | | | | | | | | | | | | | | | | | | | | | | | | |
| 27 | | | | | | | | | | | | | | | | | | | | | | | | | | | | | | |
| 28 | | | | | | | | | | | | | | | | | | | | | | | | | | | | | | |
| 29 | | | | | | | | | | | | | | | | | | | | | | | | | | | | | | |
| 30 | | | | | | | | | | | | | | | | | | | | | | | | | | | | | | |
| 31 | | | | | | | | | | | | | | | | | | | | | | | | | | | | | | |
| 32 | | | | | | | | | | | | | | | | | | | | | | | | | | | | | | |
| 33 | | | | | | | | | | | | | | | | | | | | | | | | | | | | | | |
| 34 | | | | | | | | | | | | | | | | | | | | | | | | | | | | | | |
| 35 | | | | | | | | | | | | | | | | | | | | | | | | | | | | | | |
| 36 | | | | | | | | | | | | | | | | | | | | | | | | | | | | | | |

# *Period*____________________

| Week____ | | | | | Week____ | | | | | Week____ | | | | | Week____ | | | | | Week____ | | | | | | Days Present | Days Absent | Tardies | Quarter Grade | | |
|---|---|---|---|---|---|---|---|---|---|---|---|---|---|---|---|---|---|---|---|---|---|---|---|---|---|---|---|---|---|---|---|
| M | T | W | T | F | M | T | W | T | F | M | T | W | T | F | M | T | W | T | F | M | T | W | T | F | | | | | | | |
| | | | | | | | | | | | | | | | | | | | | | | | | | 1 | | | | | | |
| | | | | | | | | | | | | | | | | | | | | | | | | | 2 | | | | | | |
| | | | | | | | | | | | | | | | | | | | | | | | | | 3 | | | | | | |
| | | | | | | | | | | | | | | | | | | | | | | | | | 4 | | | | | | |
| | | | | | | | | | | | | | | | | | | | | | | | | | 5 | | | | | | |
| | | | | | | | | | | | | | | | | | | | | | | | | | 6 | | | | | | |
| | | | | | | | | | | | | | | | | | | | | | | | | | 7 | | | | | | |
| | | | | | | | | | | | | | | | | | | | | | | | | | 8 | | | | | | |
| | | | | | | | | | | | | | | | | | | | | | | | | | 9 | | | | | | |
| | | | | | | | | | | | | | | | | | | | | | | | | | 10 | | | | | | |
| | | | | | | | | | | | | | | | | | | | | | | | | | 11 | | | | | | |
| | | | | | | | | | | | | | | | | | | | | | | | | | 12 | | | | | | |
| | | | | | | | | | | | | | | | | | | | | | | | | | 13 | | | | | | |
| | | | | | | | | | | | | | | | | | | | | | | | | | 14 | | | | | | |
| | | | | | | | | | | | | | | | | | | | | | | | | | 15 | | | | | | |
| | | | | | | | | | | | | | | | | | | | | | | | | | 16 | | | | | | |
| | | | | | | | | | | | | | | | | | | | | | | | | | 17 | | | | | | |
| | | | | | | | | | | | | | | | | | | | | | | | | | 18 | | | | | | |
| | | | | | | | | | | | | | | | | | | | | | | | | | 19 | | | | | | |
| | | | | | | | | | | | | | | | | | | | | | | | | | 20 | | | | | | |
| | | | | | | | | | | | | | | | | | | | | | | | | | 21 | | | | | | |
| | | | | | | | | | | | | | | | | | | | | | | | | | 22 | | | | | | |
| | | | | | | | | | | | | | | | | | | | | | | | | | 23 | | | | | | |
| | | | | | | | | | | | | | | | | | | | | | | | | | 24 | | | | | | |
| | | | | | | | | | | | | | | | | | | | | | | | | | 25 | | | | | | |
| | | | | | | | | | | | | | | | | | | | | | | | | | 26 | | | | | | |
| | | | | | | | | | | | | | | | | | | | | | | | | | 27 | | | | | | |
| | | | | | | | | | | | | | | | | | | | | | | | | | 28 | | | | | | |
| | | | | | | | | | | | | | | | | | | | | | | | | | 29 | | | | | | |
| | | | | | | | | | | | | | | | | | | | | | | | | | 30 | | | | | | |
| | | | | | | | | | | | | | | | | | | | | | | | | | 31 | | | | | | |
| | | | | | | | | | | | | | | | | | | | | | | | | | 32 | | | | | | |
| | | | | | | | | | | | | | | | | | | | | | | | | | 33 | | | | | | |
| | | | | | | | | | | | | | | | | | | | | | | | | | 34 | | | | | | |
| | | | | | | | | | | | | | | | | | | | | | | | | | 35 | | | | | | |
| | | | | | | | | | | | | | | | | | | | | | | | | | 36 | | | | | | |

# Subject _______________________

| Week | Week____ | | | | | Week____ | | | | | Week____ | | | | | Week____ | | | | | Week____ | | | | | Week____ | | | | |
|---|---|---|---|---|---|---|---|---|---|---|---|---|---|---|---|---|---|---|---|---|---|---|---|---|---|---|---|---|---|---|---|
| Day | M | T | W | T | F | M | T | W | T | F | M | T | W | T | F | M | T | W | T | F | M | T | W | T | F | M | T | W | T | F |
| Date | | | | | | | | | | | | | | | | | | | | | | | | | | | | | | |
| Assignments or Attendance | | | | | | | | | | | | | | | | | | | | | | | | | | | | | | |
| Name | | | | | | | | | | | | | | | | | | | | | | | | | | | | | | |
| 1 | | | | | | | | | | | | | | | | | | | | | | | | | | | | | | |
| 2 | | | | | | | | | | | | | | | | | | | | | | | | | | | | | | |
| 3 | | | | | | | | | | | | | | | | | | | | | | | | | | | | | | |
| 4 | | | | | | | | | | | | | | | | | | | | | | | | | | | | | | |
| 5 | | | | | | | | | | | | | | | | | | | | | | | | | | | | | | |
| 6 | | | | | | | | | | | | | | | | | | | | | | | | | | | | | | |
| 7 | | | | | | | | | | | | | | | | | | | | | | | | | | | | | | |
| 8 | | | | | | | | | | | | | | | | | | | | | | | | | | | | | | |
| 9 | | | | | | | | | | | | | | | | | | | | | | | | | | | | | | |
| 10 | | | | | | | | | | | | | | | | | | | | | | | | | | | | | | |
| 11 | | | | | | | | | | | | | | | | | | | | | | | | | | | | | | |
| 12 | | | | | | | | | | | | | | | | | | | | | | | | | | | | | | |
| 13 | | | | | | | | | | | | | | | | | | | | | | | | | | | | | | |
| 14 | | | | | | | | | | | | | | | | | | | | | | | | | | | | | | |
| 15 | | | | | | | | | | | | | | | | | | | | | | | | | | | | | | |
| 16 | | | | | | | | | | | | | | | | | | | | | | | | | | | | | | |
| 17 | | | | | | | | | | | | | | | | | | | | | | | | | | | | | | |
| 18 | | | | | | | | | | | | | | | | | | | | | | | | | | | | | | |
| 19 | | | | | | | | | | | | | | | | | | | | | | | | | | | | | | |
| 20 | | | | | | | | | | | | | | | | | | | | | | | | | | | | | | |
| 21 | | | | | | | | | | | | | | | | | | | | | | | | | | | | | | |
| 22 | | | | | | | | | | | | | | | | | | | | | | | | | | | | | | |
| 23 | | | | | | | | | | | | | | | | | | | | | | | | | | | | | | |
| 24 | | | | | | | | | | | | | | | | | | | | | | | | | | | | | | |
| 25 | | | | | | | | | | | | | | | | | | | | | | | | | | | | | | |
| 26 | | | | | | | | | | | | | | | | | | | | | | | | | | | | | | |
| 27 | | | | | | | | | | | | | | | | | | | | | | | | | | | | | | |
| 28 | | | | | | | | | | | | | | | | | | | | | | | | | | | | | | |
| 29 | | | | | | | | | | | | | | | | | | | | | | | | | | | | | | |
| 30 | | | | | | | | | | | | | | | | | | | | | | | | | | | | | | |
| 31 | | | | | | | | | | | | | | | | | | | | | | | | | | | | | | |
| 32 | | | | | | | | | | | | | | | | | | | | | | | | | | | | | | |
| 33 | | | | | | | | | | | | | | | | | | | | | | | | | | | | | | |
| 34 | | | | | | | | | | | | | | | | | | | | | | | | | | | | | | |
| 35 | | | | | | | | | | | | | | | | | | | | | | | | | | | | | | |
| 36 | | | | | | | | | | | | | | | | | | | | | | | | | | | | | | |

# _Period_______________________

| Week____ | | | | | Week____ | | | | | Week____ | | | | | Week____ | | | | | Week____ | | | | | | _Days Present_ | _Days Absent_ | _Tardies_ | _Quarter Grade_ | |
|---|---|---|---|---|---|---|---|---|---|---|---|---|---|---|---|---|---|---|---|---|---|---|---|---|---|---|---|---|---|
| M | T | W | T | F | M | T | W | T | F | M | T | W | T | F | M | T | W | T | F | M | T | W | T | F | | | | | | |
| | | | | | | | | | | | | | | | | | | | | | | | | | 1 | | | | | |
| | | | | | | | | | | | | | | | | | | | | | | | | | 2 | | | | | |
| | | | | | | | | | | | | | | | | | | | | | | | | | 3 | | | | | |
| | | | | | | | | | | | | | | | | | | | | | | | | | 4 | | | | | |
| | | | | | | | | | | | | | | | | | | | | | | | | | 5 | | | | | |
| | | | | | | | | | | | | | | | | | | | | | | | | | 6 | | | | | |
| | | | | | | | | | | | | | | | | | | | | | | | | | 7 | | | | | |
| | | | | | | | | | | | | | | | | | | | | | | | | | 8 | | | | | |
| | | | | | | | | | | | | | | | | | | | | | | | | | 9 | | | | | |
| | | | | | | | | | | | | | | | | | | | | | | | | | 10 | | | | | |
| | | | | | | | | | | | | | | | | | | | | | | | | | 11 | | | | | |
| | | | | | | | | | | | | | | | | | | | | | | | | | 12 | | | | | |
| | | | | | | | | | | | | | | | | | | | | | | | | | 13 | | | | | |
| | | | | | | | | | | | | | | | | | | | | | | | | | 14 | | | | | |
| | | | | | | | | | | | | | | | | | | | | | | | | | 15 | | | | | |
| | | | | | | | | | | | | | | | | | | | | | | | | | 16 | | | | | |
| | | | | | | | | | | | | | | | | | | | | | | | | | 17 | | | | | |
| | | | | | | | | | | | | | | | | | | | | | | | | | 18 | | | | | |
| | | | | | | | | | | | | | | | | | | | | | | | | | 19 | | | | | |
| | | | | | | | | | | | | | | | | | | | | | | | | | 20 | | | | | |
| | | | | | | | | | | | | | | | | | | | | | | | | | 21 | | | | | |
| | | | | | | | | | | | | | | | | | | | | | | | | | 22 | | | | | |
| | | | | | | | | | | | | | | | | | | | | | | | | | 23 | | | | | |
| | | | | | | | | | | | | | | | | | | | | | | | | | 24 | | | | | |
| | | | | | | | | | | | | | | | | | | | | | | | | | 25 | | | | | |
| | | | | | | | | | | | | | | | | | | | | | | | | | 26 | | | | | |
| | | | | | | | | | | | | | | | | | | | | | | | | | 27 | | | | | |
| | | | | | | | | | | | | | | | | | | | | | | | | | 28 | | | | | |
| | | | | | | | | | | | | | | | | | | | | | | | | | 29 | | | | | |
| | | | | | | | | | | | | | | | | | | | | | | | | | 30 | | | | | |
| | | | | | | | | | | | | | | | | | | | | | | | | | 31 | | | | | |
| | | | | | | | | | | | | | | | | | | | | | | | | | 32 | | | | | |
| | | | | | | | | | | | | | | | | | | | | | | | | | 33 | | | | | |
| | | | | | | | | | | | | | | | | | | | | | | | | | 34 | | | | | |
| | | | | | | | | | | | | | | | | | | | | | | | | | 35 | | | | | |
| | | | | | | | | | | | | | | | | | | | | | | | | | 36 | | | | | |

# $S$ubject_______________________

| Week | Week____ | | | | | Week____ | | | | | Week____ | | | | | Week____ | | | | | Week____ | | | | | Week____ | | | | |
|---|---|---|---|---|---|---|---|---|---|---|---|---|---|---|---|---|---|---|---|---|---|---|---|---|---|---|---|---|---|---|
| Day | M | T | W | T | F | M | T | W | T | F | M | T | W | T | F | M | T | W | T | F | M | T | W | T | F | M | T | W | T | F |
| Date | | | | | | | | | | | | | | | | | | | | | | | | | | | | | | |
| Assignments or Attendance | | | | | | | | | | | | | | | | | | | | | | | | | | | | | | |
| Name | | | | | | | | | | | | | | | | | | | | | | | | | | | | | | |
| 1 | | | | | | | | | | | | | | | | | | | | | | | | | | | | | | |
| 2 | | | | | | | | | | | | | | | | | | | | | | | | | | | | | | |
| 3 | | | | | | | | | | | | | | | | | | | | | | | | | | | | | | |
| 4 | | | | | | | | | | | | | | | | | | | | | | | | | | | | | | |
| 5 | | | | | | | | | | | | | | | | | | | | | | | | | | | | | | |
| 6 | | | | | | | | | | | | | | | | | | | | | | | | | | | | | | |
| 7 | | | | | | | | | | | | | | | | | | | | | | | | | | | | | | |
| 8 | | | | | | | | | | | | | | | | | | | | | | | | | | | | | | |
| 9 | | | | | | | | | | | | | | | | | | | | | | | | | | | | | | |
| 10 | | | | | | | | | | | | | | | | | | | | | | | | | | | | | | |
| 11 | | | | | | | | | | | | | | | | | | | | | | | | | | | | | | |
| 12 | | | | | | | | | | | | | | | | | | | | | | | | | | | | | | |
| 13 | | | | | | | | | | | | | | | | | | | | | | | | | | | | | | |
| 14 | | | | | | | | | | | | | | | | | | | | | | | | | | | | | | |
| 15 | | | | | | | | | | | | | | | | | | | | | | | | | | | | | | |
| 16 | | | | | | | | | | | | | | | | | | | | | | | | | | | | | | |
| 17 | | | | | | | | | | | | | | | | | | | | | | | | | | | | | | |
| 18 | | | | | | | | | | | | | | | | | | | | | | | | | | | | | | |
| 19 | | | | | | | | | | | | | | | | | | | | | | | | | | | | | | |
| 20 | | | | | | | | | | | | | | | | | | | | | | | | | | | | | | |
| 21 | | | | | | | | | | | | | | | | | | | | | | | | | | | | | | |
| 22 | | | | | | | | | | | | | | | | | | | | | | | | | | | | | | |
| 23 | | | | | | | | | | | | | | | | | | | | | | | | | | | | | | |
| 24 | | | | | | | | | | | | | | | | | | | | | | | | | | | | | | |
| 25 | | | | | | | | | | | | | | | | | | | | | | | | | | | | | | |
| 26 | | | | | | | | | | | | | | | | | | | | | | | | | | | | | | |
| 27 | | | | | | | | | | | | | | | | | | | | | | | | | | | | | | |
| 28 | | | | | | | | | | | | | | | | | | | | | | | | | | | | | | |
| 29 | | | | | | | | | | | | | | | | | | | | | | | | | | | | | | |
| 30 | | | | | | | | | | | | | | | | | | | | | | | | | | | | | | |
| 31 | | | | | | | | | | | | | | | | | | | | | | | | | | | | | | |
| 32 | | | | | | | | | | | | | | | | | | | | | | | | | | | | | | |
| 33 | | | | | | | | | | | | | | | | | | | | | | | | | | | | | | |
| 34 | | | | | | | | | | | | | | | | | | | | | | | | | | | | | | |
| 35 | | | | | | | | | | | | | | | | | | | | | | | | | | | | | | |
| 36 | | | | | | | | | | | | | | | | | | | | | | | | | | | | | | |

# *Period* _______________________

| Week____ | | | | | Week____ | | | | | Week____ | | | | | Week____ | | | | | Week____ | | | | | | Days Present | Days Absent | Tardies | Quarter Grade | |
|---|---|---|---|---|---|---|---|---|---|---|---|---|---|---|---|---|---|---|---|---|---|---|---|---|---|---|---|---|---|---|
| M | T | W | T | F | M | T | W | T | F | M | T | W | T | F | M | T | W | T | F | M | T | W | T | F | | | | | | |
| | | | | | | | | | | | | | | | | | | | | | | | | | | | | | | |
| | | | | | | | | | | | | | | | | | | | | | | | | | | | | | | |
| | | | | | | | | | | | | | | | | | | | | | | | | | 1 | | | | | |
| | | | | | | | | | | | | | | | | | | | | | | | | | 2 | | | | | |
| | | | | | | | | | | | | | | | | | | | | | | | | | 3 | | | | | |
| | | | | | | | | | | | | | | | | | | | | | | | | | 4 | | | | | |
| | | | | | | | | | | | | | | | | | | | | | | | | | 5 | | | | | |
| | | | | | | | | | | | | | | | | | | | | | | | | | 6 | | | | | |
| | | | | | | | | | | | | | | | | | | | | | | | | | 7 | | | | | |
| | | | | | | | | | | | | | | | | | | | | | | | | | 8 | | | | | |
| | | | | | | | | | | | | | | | | | | | | | | | | | 9 | | | | | |
| | | | | | | | | | | | | | | | | | | | | | | | | | 10 | | | | | |
| | | | | | | | | | | | | | | | | | | | | | | | | | 11 | | | | | |
| | | | | | | | | | | | | | | | | | | | | | | | | | 12 | | | | | |
| | | | | | | | | | | | | | | | | | | | | | | | | | 13 | | | | | |
| | | | | | | | | | | | | | | | | | | | | | | | | | 14 | | | | | |
| | | | | | | | | | | | | | | | | | | | | | | | | | 15 | | | | | |
| | | | | | | | | | | | | | | | | | | | | | | | | | 16 | | | | | |
| | | | | | | | | | | | | | | | | | | | | | | | | | 17 | | | | | |
| | | | | | | | | | | | | | | | | | | | | | | | | | 18 | | | | | |
| | | | | | | | | | | | | | | | | | | | | | | | | | 19 | | | | | |
| | | | | | | | | | | | | | | | | | | | | | | | | | 20 | | | | | |
| | | | | | | | | | | | | | | | | | | | | | | | | | 21 | | | | | |
| | | | | | | | | | | | | | | | | | | | | | | | | | 22 | | | | | |
| | | | | | | | | | | | | | | | | | | | | | | | | | 23 | | | | | |
| | | | | | | | | | | | | | | | | | | | | | | | | | 24 | | | | | |
| | | | | | | | | | | | | | | | | | | | | | | | | | 25 | | | | | |
| | | | | | | | | | | | | | | | | | | | | | | | | | 26 | | | | | |
| | | | | | | | | | | | | | | | | | | | | | | | | | 27 | | | | | |
| | | | | | | | | | | | | | | | | | | | | | | | | | 28 | | | | | |
| | | | | | | | | | | | | | | | | | | | | | | | | | 29 | | | | | |
| | | | | | | | | | | | | | | | | | | | | | | | | | 30 | | | | | |
| | | | | | | | | | | | | | | | | | | | | | | | | | 31 | | | | | |
| | | | | | | | | | | | | | | | | | | | | | | | | | 32 | | | | | |
| | | | | | | | | | | | | | | | | | | | | | | | | | 33 | | | | | |
| | | | | | | | | | | | | | | | | | | | | | | | | | 34 | | | | | |
| | | | | | | | | | | | | | | | | | | | | | | | | | 35 | | | | | |
| | | | | | | | | | | | | | | | | | | | | | | | | | 36 | | | | | |

# $\mathcal{S}$ubject______________________

| Week | Week____ | | | | | Week____ | | | | | Week____ | | | | | Week____ | | | | | Week____ | | | | |
|---|---|---|---|---|---|---|---|---|---|---|---|---|---|---|---|---|---|---|---|---|---|---|---|---|---|
| Day | M | T | W | T | F | M | T | W | T | F | M | T | W | T | F | M | T | W | T | F | M | T | W | T | F |
| Date | | | | | | | | | | | | | | | | | | | | | | | | | |
| Assignments or Attendance | | | | | | | | | | | | | | | | | | | | | | | | | |
| Name | | | | | | | | | | | | | | | | | | | | | | | | | |
| 1 | | | | | | | | | | | | | | | | | | | | | | | | | |
| 2 | | | | | | | | | | | | | | | | | | | | | | | | | |
| 3 | | | | | | | | | | | | | | | | | | | | | | | | | |
| 4 | | | | | | | | | | | | | | | | | | | | | | | | | |
| 5 | | | | | | | | | | | | | | | | | | | | | | | | | |
| 6 | | | | | | | | | | | | | | | | | | | | | | | | | |
| 7 | | | | | | | | | | | | | | | | | | | | | | | | | |
| 8 | | | | | | | | | | | | | | | | | | | | | | | | | |
| 9 | | | | | | | | | | | | | | | | | | | | | | | | | |
| 10 | | | | | | | | | | | | | | | | | | | | | | | | | |
| 11 | | | | | | | | | | | | | | | | | | | | | | | | | |
| 12 | | | | | | | | | | | | | | | | | | | | | | | | | |
| 13 | | | | | | | | | | | | | | | | | | | | | | | | | |
| 14 | | | | | | | | | | | | | | | | | | | | | | | | | |
| 15 | | | | | | | | | | | | | | | | | | | | | | | | | |
| 16 | | | | | | | | | | | | | | | | | | | | | | | | | |
| 17 | | | | | | | | | | | | | | | | | | | | | | | | | |
| 18 | | | | | | | | | | | | | | | | | | | | | | | | | |
| 19 | | | | | | | | | | | | | | | | | | | | | | | | | |
| 20 | | | | | | | | | | | | | | | | | | | | | | | | | |
| 21 | | | | | | | | | | | | | | | | | | | | | | | | | |
| 22 | | | | | | | | | | | | | | | | | | | | | | | | | |
| 23 | | | | | | | | | | | | | | | | | | | | | | | | | |
| 24 | | | | | | | | | | | | | | | | | | | | | | | | | |
| 25 | | | | | | | | | | | | | | | | | | | | | | | | | |
| 26 | | | | | | | | | | | | | | | | | | | | | | | | | |
| 27 | | | | | | | | | | | | | | | | | | | | | | | | | |
| 28 | | | | | | | | | | | | | | | | | | | | | | | | | |
| 29 | | | | | | | | | | | | | | | | | | | | | | | | | |
| 30 | | | | | | | | | | | | | | | | | | | | | | | | | |
| 31 | | | | | | | | | | | | | | | | | | | | | | | | | |
| 32 | | | | | | | | | | | | | | | | | | | | | | | | | |
| 33 | | | | | | | | | | | | | | | | | | | | | | | | | |
| 34 | | | | | | | | | | | | | | | | | | | | | | | | | |
| 35 | | | | | | | | | | | | | | | | | | | | | | | | | |
| 36 | | | | | | | | | | | | | | | | | | | | | | | | | |

# Period _______________________

| Week ____ | | | | | Week ____ | | | | | Week ____ | | | | | Week ____ | | | | | Week ____ | | | | | | Days Present | Days Absent | Tardies | Quarter Grade | |
|---|---|---|---|---|---|---|---|---|---|---|---|---|---|---|---|---|---|---|---|---|---|---|---|---|---|---|---|---|---|
| M | T | W | T | F | M | T | W | T | F | M | T | W | T | F | M | T | W | T | F | M | T | W | T | F | | | | | |
| | | | | | | | | | | | | | | | | | | | | | | | | | 1 | | | | |
| | | | | | | | | | | | | | | | | | | | | | | | | | 2 | | | | |
| | | | | | | | | | | | | | | | | | | | | | | | | | 3 | | | | |
| | | | | | | | | | | | | | | | | | | | | | | | | | 4 | | | | |
| | | | | | | | | | | | | | | | | | | | | | | | | | 5 | | | | |
| | | | | | | | | | | | | | | | | | | | | | | | | | 6 | | | | |
| | | | | | | | | | | | | | | | | | | | | | | | | | 7 | | | | |
| | | | | | | | | | | | | | | | | | | | | | | | | | 8 | | | | |
| | | | | | | | | | | | | | | | | | | | | | | | | | 9 | | | | |
| | | | | | | | | | | | | | | | | | | | | | | | | | 10 | | | | |
| | | | | | | | | | | | | | | | | | | | | | | | | | 11 | | | | |
| | | | | | | | | | | | | | | | | | | | | | | | | | 12 | | | | |
| | | | | | | | | | | | | | | | | | | | | | | | | | 13 | | | | |
| | | | | | | | | | | | | | | | | | | | | | | | | | 14 | | | | |
| | | | | | | | | | | | | | | | | | | | | | | | | | 15 | | | | |
| | | | | | | | | | | | | | | | | | | | | | | | | | 16 | | | | |
| | | | | | | | | | | | | | | | | | | | | | | | | | 17 | | | | |
| | | | | | | | | | | | | | | | | | | | | | | | | | 18 | | | | |
| | | | | | | | | | | | | | | | | | | | | | | | | | 19 | | | | |
| | | | | | | | | | | | | | | | | | | | | | | | | | 20 | | | | |
| | | | | | | | | | | | | | | | | | | | | | | | | | 21 | | | | |
| | | | | | | | | | | | | | | | | | | | | | | | | | 22 | | | | |
| | | | | | | | | | | | | | | | | | | | | | | | | | 23 | | | | |
| | | | | | | | | | | | | | | | | | | | | | | | | | 24 | | | | |
| | | | | | | | | | | | | | | | | | | | | | | | | | 25 | | | | |
| | | | | | | | | | | | | | | | | | | | | | | | | | 26 | | | | |
| | | | | | | | | | | | | | | | | | | | | | | | | | 27 | | | | |
| | | | | | | | | | | | | | | | | | | | | | | | | | 28 | | | | |
| | | | | | | | | | | | | | | | | | | | | | | | | | 29 | | | | |
| | | | | | | | | | | | | | | | | | | | | | | | | | 30 | | | | |
| | | | | | | | | | | | | | | | | | | | | | | | | | 31 | | | | |
| | | | | | | | | | | | | | | | | | | | | | | | | | 32 | | | | |
| | | | | | | | | | | | | | | | | | | | | | | | | | 33 | | | | |
| | | | | | | | | | | | | | | | | | | | | | | | | | 34 | | | | |
| | | | | | | | | | | | | | | | | | | | | | | | | | 35 | | | | |
| | | | | | | | | | | | | | | | | | | | | | | | | | 36 | | | | |

# $\mathcal{S}$ubject___________________________

| Week | Week____ | | | | | Week____ | | | | | Week____ | | | | | Week____ | | | | | Week____ | | | | | Week____ | | | | |
|---|---|---|---|---|---|---|---|---|---|---|---|---|---|---|---|---|---|---|---|---|---|---|---|---|---|---|---|---|---|---|
| Day | M | T | W | T | F | M | T | W | T | F | M | T | W | T | F | M | T | W | T | F | M | T | W | T | F | M | T | W | T | F |
| Date | | | | | | | | | | | | | | | | | | | | | | | | | | | | | | |
| Assignments *or* Attendance | | | | | | | | | | | | | | | | | | | | | | | | | | | | | | |
| Name | | | | | | | | | | | | | | | | | | | | | | | | | | | | | | |
| 1 | | | | | | | | | | | | | | | | | | | | | | | | | | | | | | |
| 2 | | | | | | | | | | | | | | | | | | | | | | | | | | | | | | |
| 3 | | | | | | | | | | | | | | | | | | | | | | | | | | | | | | |
| 4 | | | | | | | | | | | | | | | | | | | | | | | | | | | | | | |
| 5 | | | | | | | | | | | | | | | | | | | | | | | | | | | | | | |
| 6 | | | | | | | | | | | | | | | | | | | | | | | | | | | | | | |
| 7 | | | | | | | | | | | | | | | | | | | | | | | | | | | | | | |
| 8 | | | | | | | | | | | | | | | | | | | | | | | | | | | | | | |
| 9 | | | | | | | | | | | | | | | | | | | | | | | | | | | | | | |
| 10 | | | | | | | | | | | | | | | | | | | | | | | | | | | | | | |
| 11 | | | | | | | | | | | | | | | | | | | | | | | | | | | | | | |
| 12 | | | | | | | | | | | | | | | | | | | | | | | | | | | | | | |
| 13 | | | | | | | | | | | | | | | | | | | | | | | | | | | | | | |
| 14 | | | | | | | | | | | | | | | | | | | | | | | | | | | | | | |
| 15 | | | | | | | | | | | | | | | | | | | | | | | | | | | | | | |
| 16 | | | | | | | | | | | | | | | | | | | | | | | | | | | | | | |
| 17 | | | | | | | | | | | | | | | | | | | | | | | | | | | | | | |
| 18 | | | | | | | | | | | | | | | | | | | | | | | | | | | | | | |
| 19 | | | | | | | | | | | | | | | | | | | | | | | | | | | | | | |
| 20 | | | | | | | | | | | | | | | | | | | | | | | | | | | | | | |
| 21 | | | | | | | | | | | | | | | | | | | | | | | | | | | | | | |
| 22 | | | | | | | | | | | | | | | | | | | | | | | | | | | | | | |
| 23 | | | | | | | | | | | | | | | | | | | | | | | | | | | | | | |
| 24 | | | | | | | | | | | | | | | | | | | | | | | | | | | | | | |
| 25 | | | | | | | | | | | | | | | | | | | | | | | | | | | | | | |
| 26 | | | | | | | | | | | | | | | | | | | | | | | | | | | | | | |
| 27 | | | | | | | | | | | | | | | | | | | | | | | | | | | | | | |
| 28 | | | | | | | | | | | | | | | | | | | | | | | | | | | | | | |
| 29 | | | | | | | | | | | | | | | | | | | | | | | | | | | | | | |
| 30 | | | | | | | | | | | | | | | | | | | | | | | | | | | | | | |
| 31 | | | | | | | | | | | | | | | | | | | | | | | | | | | | | | |
| 32 | | | | | | | | | | | | | | | | | | | | | | | | | | | | | | |
| 33 | | | | | | | | | | | | | | | | | | | | | | | | | | | | | | |
| 34 | | | | | | | | | | | | | | | | | | | | | | | | | | | | | | |
| 35 | | | | | | | | | | | | | | | | | | | | | | | | | | | | | | |
| 36 | | | | | | | | | | | | | | | | | | | | | | | | | | | | | | |

# _Period_________________________

| Week____ | | | | | Week____ | | | | | Week____ | | | | | Week____ | | | | | Week____ | | | | | | Days Present | Days Absent | Tardies | Quarter Grade |
|---|---|---|---|---|---|---|---|---|---|---|---|---|---|---|---|---|---|---|---|---|---|---|---|---|---|---|---|---|---|
| M | T | W | T | F | M | T | W | T | F | M | T | W | T | F | M | T | W | T | F | M | T | W | T | F | | | | | |
| | | | | | | | | | | | | | | | | | | | | | | | | | | | | | |
| | | | | | | | | | | | | | | | | | | | | | | | | | | | | | |
| | | | | | | | | | | | | | | | | | | | | | | | | | | | | | |
| | | | | | | | | | | | | | | | | | | | | | | | | | 1 | | | | |
| | | | | | | | | | | | | | | | | | | | | | | | | | 2 | | | | |
| | | | | | | | | | | | | | | | | | | | | | | | | | 3 | | | | |
| | | | | | | | | | | | | | | | | | | | | | | | | | 4 | | | | |
| | | | | | | | | | | | | | | | | | | | | | | | | | 5 | | | | |
| | | | | | | | | | | | | | | | | | | | | | | | | | 6 | | | | |
| | | | | | | | | | | | | | | | | | | | | | | | | | 7 | | | | |
| | | | | | | | | | | | | | | | | | | | | | | | | | 8 | | | | |
| | | | | | | | | | | | | | | | | | | | | | | | | | 9 | | | | |
| | | | | | | | | | | | | | | | | | | | | | | | | | 10 | | | | |
| | | | | | | | | | | | | | | | | | | | | | | | | | 11 | | | | |
| | | | | | | | | | | | | | | | | | | | | | | | | | 12 | | | | |
| | | | | | | | | | | | | | | | | | | | | | | | | | 13 | | | | |
| | | | | | | | | | | | | | | | | | | | | | | | | | 14 | | | | |
| | | | | | | | | | | | | | | | | | | | | | | | | | 15 | | | | |
| | | | | | | | | | | | | | | | | | | | | | | | | | 16 | | | | |
| | | | | | | | | | | | | | | | | | | | | | | | | | 17 | | | | |
| | | | | | | | | | | | | | | | | | | | | | | | | | 18 | | | | |
| | | | | | | | | | | | | | | | | | | | | | | | | | 19 | | | | |
| | | | | | | | | | | | | | | | | | | | | | | | | | 20 | | | | |
| | | | | | | | | | | | | | | | | | | | | | | | | | 21 | | | | |
| | | | | | | | | | | | | | | | | | | | | | | | | | 22 | | | | |
| | | | | | | | | | | | | | | | | | | | | | | | | | 23 | | | | |
| | | | | | | | | | | | | | | | | | | | | | | | | | 24 | | | | |
| | | | | | | | | | | | | | | | | | | | | | | | | | 25 | | | | |
| | | | | | | | | | | | | | | | | | | | | | | | | | 26 | | | | |
| | | | | | | | | | | | | | | | | | | | | | | | | | 27 | | | | |
| | | | | | | | | | | | | | | | | | | | | | | | | | 28 | | | | |
| | | | | | | | | | | | | | | | | | | | | | | | | | 29 | | | | |
| | | | | | | | | | | | | | | | | | | | | | | | | | 30 | | | | |
| | | | | | | | | | | | | | | | | | | | | | | | | | 31 | | | | |
| | | | | | | | | | | | | | | | | | | | | | | | | | 32 | | | | |
| | | | | | | | | | | | | | | | | | | | | | | | | | 33 | | | | |
| | | | | | | | | | | | | | | | | | | | | | | | | | 34 | | | | |
| | | | | | | | | | | | | | | | | | | | | | | | | | 35 | | | | |
| | | | | | | | | | | | | | | | | | | | | | | | | | 36 | | | | |

# $\mathcal{S}$ubject______________________

| Week | Week____ | | | | | Week____ | | | | | Week____ | | | | | Week____ | | | | | Week____ | | | | | Week____ | | | | |
|---|---|---|---|---|---|---|---|---|---|---|---|---|---|---|---|---|---|---|---|---|---|---|---|---|---|---|---|---|---|---|
| Day | M | T | W | T | F | M | T | W | T | F | M | T | W | T | F | M | T | W | T | F | M | T | W | T | F | M | T | W | T | F |
| Date | | | | | | | | | | | | | | | | | | | | | | | | | | | | | | |
| Assignments or Attendance | | | | | | | | | | | | | | | | | | | | | | | | | | | | | | |
| Name | | | | | | | | | | | | | | | | | | | | | | | | | | | | | | |
| 1 | | | | | | | | | | | | | | | | | | | | | | | | | | | | | | |
| 2 | | | | | | | | | | | | | | | | | | | | | | | | | | | | | | |
| 3 | | | | | | | | | | | | | | | | | | | | | | | | | | | | | | |
| 4 | | | | | | | | | | | | | | | | | | | | | | | | | | | | | | |
| 5 | | | | | | | | | | | | | | | | | | | | | | | | | | | | | | |
| 6 | | | | | | | | | | | | | | | | | | | | | | | | | | | | | | |
| 7 | | | | | | | | | | | | | | | | | | | | | | | | | | | | | | |
| 8 | | | | | | | | | | | | | | | | | | | | | | | | | | | | | | |
| 9 | | | | | | | | | | | | | | | | | | | | | | | | | | | | | | |
| 10 | | | | | | | | | | | | | | | | | | | | | | | | | | | | | | |
| 11 | | | | | | | | | | | | | | | | | | | | | | | | | | | | | | |
| 12 | | | | | | | | | | | | | | | | | | | | | | | | | | | | | | |
| 13 | | | | | | | | | | | | | | | | | | | | | | | | | | | | | | |
| 14 | | | | | | | | | | | | | | | | | | | | | | | | | | | | | | |
| 15 | | | | | | | | | | | | | | | | | | | | | | | | | | | | | | |
| 16 | | | | | | | | | | | | | | | | | | | | | | | | | | | | | | |
| 17 | | | | | | | | | | | | | | | | | | | | | | | | | | | | | | |
| 18 | | | | | | | | | | | | | | | | | | | | | | | | | | | | | | |
| 19 | | | | | | | | | | | | | | | | | | | | | | | | | | | | | | |
| 20 | | | | | | | | | | | | | | | | | | | | | | | | | | | | | | |
| 21 | | | | | | | | | | | | | | | | | | | | | | | | | | | | | | |
| 22 | | | | | | | | | | | | | | | | | | | | | | | | | | | | | | |
| 23 | | | | | | | | | | | | | | | | | | | | | | | | | | | | | | |
| 24 | | | | | | | | | | | | | | | | | | | | | | | | | | | | | | |
| 25 | | | | | | | | | | | | | | | | | | | | | | | | | | | | | | |
| 26 | | | | | | | | | | | | | | | | | | | | | | | | | | | | | | |
| 27 | | | | | | | | | | | | | | | | | | | | | | | | | | | | | | |
| 28 | | | | | | | | | | | | | | | | | | | | | | | | | | | | | | |
| 29 | | | | | | | | | | | | | | | | | | | | | | | | | | | | | | |
| 30 | | | | | | | | | | | | | | | | | | | | | | | | | | | | | | |
| 31 | | | | | | | | | | | | | | | | | | | | | | | | | | | | | | |
| 32 | | | | | | | | | | | | | | | | | | | | | | | | | | | | | | |
| 33 | | | | | | | | | | | | | | | | | | | | | | | | | | | | | | |
| 34 | | | | | | | | | | | | | | | | | | | | | | | | | | | | | | |
| 35 | | | | | | | | | | | | | | | | | | | | | | | | | | | | | | |
| 36 | | | | | | | | | | | | | | | | | | | | | | | | | | | | | | |

# Period_______________________

| Week____ | | | | | Week____ | | | | | Week____ | | | | | Week____ | | | | | Week____ | | | | | Days Present | Days Absent | Tardies | Quarter Grade | |
|---|---|---|---|---|---|---|---|---|---|---|---|---|---|---|---|---|---|---|---|---|---|---|---|---|---|---|---|---|
| M | T | W | T | F | M | T | W | T | F | M | T | W | T | F | M | T | W | T | F | M | T | W | T | F | | | | | |
| | | | | | | | | | | | | | | | | | | | | | | | | | | | | | |
| | | | | | | | | | | | | | | | | | | | | | | | | | 1 | | | | |
| | | | | | | | | | | | | | | | | | | | | | | | | | 2 | | | | |
| | | | | | | | | | | | | | | | | | | | | | | | | | 3 | | | | |
| | | | | | | | | | | | | | | | | | | | | | | | | | 4 | | | | |
| | | | | | | | | | | | | | | | | | | | | | | | | | 5 | | | | |
| | | | | | | | | | | | | | | | | | | | | | | | | | 6 | | | | |
| | | | | | | | | | | | | | | | | | | | | | | | | | 7 | | | | |
| | | | | | | | | | | | | | | | | | | | | | | | | | 8 | | | | |
| | | | | | | | | | | | | | | | | | | | | | | | | | 9 | | | | |
| | | | | | | | | | | | | | | | | | | | | | | | | | 10 | | | | |
| | | | | | | | | | | | | | | | | | | | | | | | | | 11 | | | | |
| | | | | | | | | | | | | | | | | | | | | | | | | | 12 | | | | |
| | | | | | | | | | | | | | | | | | | | | | | | | | 13 | | | | |
| | | | | | | | | | | | | | | | | | | | | | | | | | 14 | | | | |
| | | | | | | | | | | | | | | | | | | | | | | | | | 15 | | | | |
| | | | | | | | | | | | | | | | | | | | | | | | | | 16 | | | | |
| | | | | | | | | | | | | | | | | | | | | | | | | | 17 | | | | |
| | | | | | | | | | | | | | | | | | | | | | | | | | 18 | | | | |
| | | | | | | | | | | | | | | | | | | | | | | | | | 19 | | | | |
| | | | | | | | | | | | | | | | | | | | | | | | | | 20 | | | | |
| | | | | | | | | | | | | | | | | | | | | | | | | | 21 | | | | |
| | | | | | | | | | | | | | | | | | | | | | | | | | 22 | | | | |
| | | | | | | | | | | | | | | | | | | | | | | | | | 23 | | | | |
| | | | | | | | | | | | | | | | | | | | | | | | | | 24 | | | | |
| | | | | | | | | | | | | | | | | | | | | | | | | | 25 | | | | |
| | | | | | | | | | | | | | | | | | | | | | | | | | 26 | | | | |
| | | | | | | | | | | | | | | | | | | | | | | | | | 27 | | | | |
| | | | | | | | | | | | | | | | | | | | | | | | | | 28 | | | | |
| | | | | | | | | | | | | | | | | | | | | | | | | | 29 | | | | |
| | | | | | | | | | | | | | | | | | | | | | | | | | 30 | | | | |
| | | | | | | | | | | | | | | | | | | | | | | | | | 31 | | | | |
| | | | | | | | | | | | | | | | | | | | | | | | | | 32 | | | | |
| | | | | | | | | | | | | | | | | | | | | | | | | | 33 | | | | |
| | | | | | | | | | | | | | | | | | | | | | | | | | 34 | | | | |
| | | | | | | | | | | | | | | | | | | | | | | | | | 35 | | | | |
| | | | | | | | | | | | | | | | | | | | | | | | | | 36 | | | | |

# $\mathcal{S}$ubject_______________________

| Week | Week____ | | | | | Week____ | | | | | Week____ | | | | | Week____ | | | | | Week____ | | | | | Week____ | | | | |
|---|---|---|---|---|---|---|---|---|---|---|---|---|---|---|---|---|---|---|---|---|---|---|---|---|---|---|
| Day | M | T | W | T | F | M | T | W | T | F | M | T | W | T | F | M | T | W | T | F | M | T | W | T | F | M | T | W | T | F |
| Date | | | | | | | | | | | | | | | | | | | | | | | | | | | | | | |
| Assignments or Attendance | | | | | | | | | | | | | | | | | | | | | | | | | | | | | | |
| Name | | | | | | | | | | | | | | | | | | | | | | | | | | | | | | |
| 1 | | | | | | | | | | | | | | | | | | | | | | | | | | | | | | |
| 2 | | | | | | | | | | | | | | | | | | | | | | | | | | | | | | |
| 3 | | | | | | | | | | | | | | | | | | | | | | | | | | | | | | |
| 4 | | | | | | | | | | | | | | | | | | | | | | | | | | | | | | |
| 5 | | | | | | | | | | | | | | | | | | | | | | | | | | | | | | |
| 6 | | | | | | | | | | | | | | | | | | | | | | | | | | | | | | |
| 7 | | | | | | | | | | | | | | | | | | | | | | | | | | | | | | |
| 8 | | | | | | | | | | | | | | | | | | | | | | | | | | | | | | |
| 9 | | | | | | | | | | | | | | | | | | | | | | | | | | | | | | |
| 10 | | | | | | | | | | | | | | | | | | | | | | | | | | | | | | |
| 11 | | | | | | | | | | | | | | | | | | | | | | | | | | | | | | |
| 12 | | | | | | | | | | | | | | | | | | | | | | | | | | | | | | |
| 13 | | | | | | | | | | | | | | | | | | | | | | | | | | | | | | |
| 14 | | | | | | | | | | | | | | | | | | | | | | | | | | | | | | |
| 15 | | | | | | | | | | | | | | | | | | | | | | | | | | | | | | |
| 16 | | | | | | | | | | | | | | | | | | | | | | | | | | | | | | |
| 17 | | | | | | | | | | | | | | | | | | | | | | | | | | | | | | |
| 18 | | | | | | | | | | | | | | | | | | | | | | | | | | | | | | |
| 19 | | | | | | | | | | | | | | | | | | | | | | | | | | | | | | |
| 20 | | | | | | | | | | | | | | | | | | | | | | | | | | | | | | |
| 21 | | | | | | | | | | | | | | | | | | | | | | | | | | | | | | |
| 22 | | | | | | | | | | | | | | | | | | | | | | | | | | | | | | |
| 23 | | | | | | | | | | | | | | | | | | | | | | | | | | | | | | |
| 24 | | | | | | | | | | | | | | | | | | | | | | | | | | | | | | |
| 25 | | | | | | | | | | | | | | | | | | | | | | | | | | | | | | |
| 26 | | | | | | | | | | | | | | | | | | | | | | | | | | | | | | |
| 27 | | | | | | | | | | | | | | | | | | | | | | | | | | | | | | |
| 28 | | | | | | | | | | | | | | | | | | | | | | | | | | | | | | |
| 29 | | | | | | | | | | | | | | | | | | | | | | | | | | | | | | |
| 30 | | | | | | | | | | | | | | | | | | | | | | | | | | | | | | |
| 31 | | | | | | | | | | | | | | | | | | | | | | | | | | | | | | |
| 32 | | | | | | | | | | | | | | | | | | | | | | | | | | | | | | |
| 33 | | | | | | | | | | | | | | | | | | | | | | | | | | | | | | |
| 34 | | | | | | | | | | | | | | | | | | | | | | | | | | | | | | |
| 35 | | | | | | | | | | | | | | | | | | | | | | | | | | | | | | |
| 36 | | | | | | | | | | | | | | | | | | | | | | | | | | | | | | |

# Period_____________________

| Week____ | | | | | Week____ | | | | | Week____ | | | | | Week____ | | | | | Week____ | | | | | | Days Present | Days Absent | Tardies | Quarter Grade | |
|---|---|---|---|---|---|---|---|---|---|---|---|---|---|---|---|---|---|---|---|---|---|---|---|---|---|---|---|---|---|---|
| M | T | W | T | F | M | T | W | T | F | M | T | W | T | F | M | T | W | T | F | M | T | W | T | F | | | | | | |
| | | | | | | | | | | | | | | | | | | | | | | | | | 1 | | | | | |
| | | | | | | | | | | | | | | | | | | | | | | | | | 2 | | | | | |
| | | | | | | | | | | | | | | | | | | | | | | | | | 3 | | | | | |
| | | | | | | | | | | | | | | | | | | | | | | | | | 4 | | | | | |
| | | | | | | | | | | | | | | | | | | | | | | | | | 5 | | | | | |
| | | | | | | | | | | | | | | | | | | | | | | | | | 6 | | | | | |
| | | | | | | | | | | | | | | | | | | | | | | | | | 7 | | | | | |
| | | | | | | | | | | | | | | | | | | | | | | | | | 8 | | | | | |
| | | | | | | | | | | | | | | | | | | | | | | | | | 9 | | | | | |
| | | | | | | | | | | | | | | | | | | | | | | | | | 10 | | | | | |
| | | | | | | | | | | | | | | | | | | | | | | | | | 11 | | | | | |
| | | | | | | | | | | | | | | | | | | | | | | | | | 12 | | | | | |
| | | | | | | | | | | | | | | | | | | | | | | | | | 13 | | | | | |
| | | | | | | | | | | | | | | | | | | | | | | | | | 14 | | | | | |
| | | | | | | | | | | | | | | | | | | | | | | | | | 15 | | | | | |
| | | | | | | | | | | | | | | | | | | | | | | | | | 16 | | | | | |
| | | | | | | | | | | | | | | | | | | | | | | | | | 17 | | | | | |
| | | | | | | | | | | | | | | | | | | | | | | | | | 18 | | | | | |
| | | | | | | | | | | | | | | | | | | | | | | | | | 19 | | | | | |
| | | | | | | | | | | | | | | | | | | | | | | | | | 20 | | | | | |
| | | | | | | | | | | | | | | | | | | | | | | | | | 21 | | | | | |
| | | | | | | | | | | | | | | | | | | | | | | | | | 22 | | | | | |
| | | | | | | | | | | | | | | | | | | | | | | | | | 23 | | | | | |
| | | | | | | | | | | | | | | | | | | | | | | | | | 24 | | | | | |
| | | | | | | | | | | | | | | | | | | | | | | | | | 25 | | | | | |
| | | | | | | | | | | | | | | | | | | | | | | | | | 26 | | | | | |
| | | | | | | | | | | | | | | | | | | | | | | | | | 27 | | | | | |
| | | | | | | | | | | | | | | | | | | | | | | | | | 28 | | | | | |
| | | | | | | | | | | | | | | | | | | | | | | | | | 29 | | | | | |
| | | | | | | | | | | | | | | | | | | | | | | | | | 30 | | | | | |
| | | | | | | | | | | | | | | | | | | | | | | | | | 31 | | | | | |
| | | | | | | | | | | | | | | | | | | | | | | | | | 32 | | | | | |
| | | | | | | | | | | | | | | | | | | | | | | | | | 33 | | | | | |
| | | | | | | | | | | | | | | | | | | | | | | | | | 34 | | | | | |
| | | | | | | | | | | | | | | | | | | | | | | | | | 35 | | | | | |
| | | | | | | | | | | | | | | | | | | | | | | | | | 36 | | | | | |

# Subject _______________________

| Week | Week____ | | | | | Week____ | | | | | Week____ | | | | | Week____ | | | | | Week____ | | | | | Week____ | | | | |
|---|---|---|---|---|---|---|---|---|---|---|---|---|---|---|---|---|---|---|---|---|---|---|---|---|---|
| Day | M | T | W | T | F | M | T | W | T | F | M | T | W | T | F | M | T | W | T | F | M | T | W | T | F |
| Date | | | | | | | | | | | | | | | | | | | | | | | | | |
| Assignments or Attendance | | | | | | | | | | | | | | | | | | | | | | | | | |
| Name | | | | | | | | | | | | | | | | | | | | | | | | | |
| 1 | | | | | | | | | | | | | | | | | | | | | | | | | |
| 2 | | | | | | | | | | | | | | | | | | | | | | | | | |
| 3 | | | | | | | | | | | | | | | | | | | | | | | | | |
| 4 | | | | | | | | | | | | | | | | | | | | | | | | | |
| 5 | | | | | | | | | | | | | | | | | | | | | | | | | |
| 6 | | | | | | | | | | | | | | | | | | | | | | | | | |
| 7 | | | | | | | | | | | | | | | | | | | | | | | | | |
| 8 | | | | | | | | | | | | | | | | | | | | | | | | | |
| 9 | | | | | | | | | | | | | | | | | | | | | | | | | |
| 10 | | | | | | | | | | | | | | | | | | | | | | | | | |
| 11 | | | | | | | | | | | | | | | | | | | | | | | | | |
| 12 | | | | | | | | | | | | | | | | | | | | | | | | | |
| 13 | | | | | | | | | | | | | | | | | | | | | | | | | |
| 14 | | | | | | | | | | | | | | | | | | | | | | | | | |
| 15 | | | | | | | | | | | | | | | | | | | | | | | | | |
| 16 | | | | | | | | | | | | | | | | | | | | | | | | | |
| 17 | | | | | | | | | | | | | | | | | | | | | | | | | |
| 18 | | | | | | | | | | | | | | | | | | | | | | | | | |
| 19 | | | | | | | | | | | | | | | | | | | | | | | | | |
| 20 | | | | | | | | | | | | | | | | | | | | | | | | | |
| 21 | | | | | | | | | | | | | | | | | | | | | | | | | |
| 22 | | | | | | | | | | | | | | | | | | | | | | | | | |
| 23 | | | | | | | | | | | | | | | | | | | | | | | | | |
| 24 | | | | | | | | | | | | | | | | | | | | | | | | | |
| 25 | | | | | | | | | | | | | | | | | | | | | | | | | |
| 26 | | | | | | | | | | | | | | | | | | | | | | | | | |
| 27 | | | | | | | | | | | | | | | | | | | | | | | | | |
| 28 | | | | | | | | | | | | | | | | | | | | | | | | | |
| 29 | | | | | | | | | | | | | | | | | | | | | | | | | |
| 30 | | | | | | | | | | | | | | | | | | | | | | | | | |
| 31 | | | | | | | | | | | | | | | | | | | | | | | | | |
| 32 | | | | | | | | | | | | | | | | | | | | | | | | | |
| 33 | | | | | | | | | | | | | | | | | | | | | | | | | |
| 34 | | | | | | | | | | | | | | | | | | | | | | | | | |
| 35 | | | | | | | | | | | | | | | | | | | | | | | | | |
| 36 | | | | | | | | | | | | | | | | | | | | | | | | | |

# *Period*___________________________

| Week____ | | | | | Week____ | | | | | Week____ | | | | | Week____ | | | | | Week____ | | | | | | Days Present | Days Absent | Tardies | Quarter Grade | | |
|---|---|---|---|---|---|---|---|---|---|---|---|---|---|---|---|---|---|---|---|---|---|---|---|---|---|---|---|---|---|---|
| M | T | W | T | F | M | T | W | T | F | M | T | W | T | F | M | T | W | T | F | M | T | W | T | F | | | | | | |
| | | | | | | | | | | | | | | | | | | | | | | | | | 1 | | | | | | |
| | | | | | | | | | | | | | | | | | | | | | | | | | 2 | | | | | | |
| | | | | | | | | | | | | | | | | | | | | | | | | | 3 | | | | | | |
| | | | | | | | | | | | | | | | | | | | | | | | | | 4 | | | | | | |
| | | | | | | | | | | | | | | | | | | | | | | | | | 5 | | | | | | |
| | | | | | | | | | | | | | | | | | | | | | | | | | 6 | | | | | | |
| | | | | | | | | | | | | | | | | | | | | | | | | | 7 | | | | | | |
| | | | | | | | | | | | | | | | | | | | | | | | | | 8 | | | | | | |
| | | | | | | | | | | | | | | | | | | | | | | | | | 9 | | | | | | |
| | | | | | | | | | | | | | | | | | | | | | | | | | 10 | | | | | | |
| | | | | | | | | | | | | | | | | | | | | | | | | | 11 | | | | | | |
| | | | | | | | | | | | | | | | | | | | | | | | | | 12 | | | | | | |
| | | | | | | | | | | | | | | | | | | | | | | | | | 13 | | | | | | |
| | | | | | | | | | | | | | | | | | | | | | | | | | 14 | | | | | | |
| | | | | | | | | | | | | | | | | | | | | | | | | | 15 | | | | | | |
| | | | | | | | | | | | | | | | | | | | | | | | | | 16 | | | | | | |
| | | | | | | | | | | | | | | | | | | | | | | | | | 17 | | | | | | |
| | | | | | | | | | | | | | | | | | | | | | | | | | 18 | | | | | | |
| | | | | | | | | | | | | | | | | | | | | | | | | | 19 | | | | | | |
| | | | | | | | | | | | | | | | | | | | | | | | | | 20 | | | | | | |
| | | | | | | | | | | | | | | | | | | | | | | | | | 21 | | | | | | |
| | | | | | | | | | | | | | | | | | | | | | | | | | 22 | | | | | | |
| | | | | | | | | | | | | | | | | | | | | | | | | | 23 | | | | | | |
| | | | | | | | | | | | | | | | | | | | | | | | | | 24 | | | | | | |
| | | | | | | | | | | | | | | | | | | | | | | | | | 25 | | | | | | |
| | | | | | | | | | | | | | | | | | | | | | | | | | 26 | | | | | | |
| | | | | | | | | | | | | | | | | | | | | | | | | | 27 | | | | | | |
| | | | | | | | | | | | | | | | | | | | | | | | | | 28 | | | | | | |
| | | | | | | | | | | | | | | | | | | | | | | | | | 29 | | | | | | |
| | | | | | | | | | | | | | | | | | | | | | | | | | 30 | | | | | | |
| | | | | | | | | | | | | | | | | | | | | | | | | | 31 | | | | | | |
| | | | | | | | | | | | | | | | | | | | | | | | | | 32 | | | | | | |
| | | | | | | | | | | | | | | | | | | | | | | | | | 33 | | | | | | |
| | | | | | | | | | | | | | | | | | | | | | | | | | 34 | | | | | | |
| | | | | | | | | | | | | | | | | | | | | | | | | | 35 | | | | | | |
| | | | | | | | | | | | | | | | | | | | | | | | | | 36 | | | | | | |

# $\mathcal{S}$ubject________________________

| Week | Week____ | | | | | Week____ | | | | | Week____ | | | | | Week____ | | | | | Week____ | | | | | Week____ | | | | |
|---|---|---|---|---|---|---|---|---|---|---|---|---|---|---|---|---|---|---|---|---|---|---|---|---|---|---|---|---|---|---|
| Day | M | T | W | T | F | M | T | W | T | F | M | T | W | T | F | M | T | W | T | F | M | T | W | T | F | M | T | W | T | F |
| Date | | | | | | | | | | | | | | | | | | | | | | | | | | | | | | |
| *Assignments or Attendance* | | | | | | | | | | | | | | | | | | | | | | | | | | | | | | |
| *Name* | | | | | | | | | | | | | | | | | | | | | | | | | | | | | | |
| 1 | | | | | | | | | | | | | | | | | | | | | | | | | | | | | | |
| 2 | | | | | | | | | | | | | | | | | | | | | | | | | | | | | | |
| 3 | | | | | | | | | | | | | | | | | | | | | | | | | | | | | | |
| 4 | | | | | | | | | | | | | | | | | | | | | | | | | | | | | | |
| 5 | | | | | | | | | | | | | | | | | | | | | | | | | | | | | | |
| 6 | | | | | | | | | | | | | | | | | | | | | | | | | | | | | | |
| 7 | | | | | | | | | | | | | | | | | | | | | | | | | | | | | | |
| 8 | | | | | | | | | | | | | | | | | | | | | | | | | | | | | | |
| 9 | | | | | | | | | | | | | | | | | | | | | | | | | | | | | | |
| 10 | | | | | | | | | | | | | | | | | | | | | | | | | | | | | | |
| 11 | | | | | | | | | | | | | | | | | | | | | | | | | | | | | | |
| 12 | | | | | | | | | | | | | | | | | | | | | | | | | | | | | | |
| 13 | | | | | | | | | | | | | | | | | | | | | | | | | | | | | | |
| 14 | | | | | | | | | | | | | | | | | | | | | | | | | | | | | | |
| 15 | | | | | | | | | | | | | | | | | | | | | | | | | | | | | | |
| 16 | | | | | | | | | | | | | | | | | | | | | | | | | | | | | | |
| 17 | | | | | | | | | | | | | | | | | | | | | | | | | | | | | | |
| 18 | | | | | | | | | | | | | | | | | | | | | | | | | | | | | | |
| 19 | | | | | | | | | | | | | | | | | | | | | | | | | | | | | | |
| 20 | | | | | | | | | | | | | | | | | | | | | | | | | | | | | | |
| 21 | | | | | | | | | | | | | | | | | | | | | | | | | | | | | | |
| 22 | | | | | | | | | | | | | | | | | | | | | | | | | | | | | | |
| 23 | | | | | | | | | | | | | | | | | | | | | | | | | | | | | | |
| 24 | | | | | | | | | | | | | | | | | | | | | | | | | | | | | | |
| 25 | | | | | | | | | | | | | | | | | | | | | | | | | | | | | | |
| 26 | | | | | | | | | | | | | | | | | | | | | | | | | | | | | | |
| 27 | | | | | | | | | | | | | | | | | | | | | | | | | | | | | | |
| 28 | | | | | | | | | | | | | | | | | | | | | | | | | | | | | | |
| 29 | | | | | | | | | | | | | | | | | | | | | | | | | | | | | | |
| 30 | | | | | | | | | | | | | | | | | | | | | | | | | | | | | | |
| 31 | | | | | | | | | | | | | | | | | | | | | | | | | | | | | | |
| 32 | | | | | | | | | | | | | | | | | | | | | | | | | | | | | | |
| 33 | | | | | | | | | | | | | | | | | | | | | | | | | | | | | | |
| 34 | | | | | | | | | | | | | | | | | | | | | | | | | | | | | | |
| 35 | | | | | | | | | | | | | | | | | | | | | | | | | | | | | | |
| 36 | | | | | | | | | | | | | | | | | | | | | | | | | | | | | | |

| Week____ | | | | | Week____ | | | | | Week____ | | | | | Week____ | | | | | Week____ | | | | | | Days Present | Days Absent | Tardies | Quarter Grade | |
|---|---|---|---|---|---|---|---|---|---|---|---|---|---|---|---|---|---|---|---|---|---|---|---|---|---|---|---|---|---|---|
| M | T | W | T | F | M | T | W | T | F | M | T | W | T | F | M | T | W | T | F | M | T | W | T | F | | | | | | |
| | | | | | | | | | | | | | | | | | | | | | | | | | 1 | | | | | |
| | | | | | | | | | | | | | | | | | | | | | | | | | 2 | | | | | |
| | | | | | | | | | | | | | | | | | | | | | | | | | 3 | | | | | |
| | | | | | | | | | | | | | | | | | | | | | | | | | 4 | | | | | |
| | | | | | | | | | | | | | | | | | | | | | | | | | 5 | | | | | |
| | | | | | | | | | | | | | | | | | | | | | | | | | 6 | | | | | |
| | | | | | | | | | | | | | | | | | | | | | | | | | 7 | | | | | |
| | | | | | | | | | | | | | | | | | | | | | | | | | 8 | | | | | |
| | | | | | | | | | | | | | | | | | | | | | | | | | 9 | | | | | |
| | | | | | | | | | | | | | | | | | | | | | | | | | 10 | | | | | |
| | | | | | | | | | | | | | | | | | | | | | | | | | 11 | | | | | |
| | | | | | | | | | | | | | | | | | | | | | | | | | 12 | | | | | |
| | | | | | | | | | | | | | | | | | | | | | | | | | 13 | | | | | |
| | | | | | | | | | | | | | | | | | | | | | | | | | 14 | | | | | |
| | | | | | | | | | | | | | | | | | | | | | | | | | 15 | | | | | |
| | | | | | | | | | | | | | | | | | | | | | | | | | 16 | | | | | |
| | | | | | | | | | | | | | | | | | | | | | | | | | 17 | | | | | |
| | | | | | | | | | | | | | | | | | | | | | | | | | 18 | | | | | |
| | | | | | | | | | | | | | | | | | | | | | | | | | 19 | | | | | |
| | | | | | | | | | | | | | | | | | | | | | | | | | 20 | | | | | |
| | | | | | | | | | | | | | | | | | | | | | | | | | 21 | | | | | |
| | | | | | | | | | | | | | | | | | | | | | | | | | 22 | | | | | |
| | | | | | | | | | | | | | | | | | | | | | | | | | 23 | | | | | |
| | | | | | | | | | | | | | | | | | | | | | | | | | 24 | | | | | |
| | | | | | | | | | | | | | | | | | | | | | | | | | 25 | | | | | |
| | | | | | | | | | | | | | | | | | | | | | | | | | 26 | | | | | |
| | | | | | | | | | | | | | | | | | | | | | | | | | 27 | | | | | |
| | | | | | | | | | | | | | | | | | | | | | | | | | 28 | | | | | |
| | | | | | | | | | | | | | | | | | | | | | | | | | 29 | | | | | |
| | | | | | | | | | | | | | | | | | | | | | | | | | 30 | | | | | |
| | | | | | | | | | | | | | | | | | | | | | | | | | 31 | | | | | |
| | | | | | | | | | | | | | | | | | | | | | | | | | 32 | | | | | |
| | | | | | | | | | | | | | | | | | | | | | | | | | 33 | | | | | |
| | | | | | | | | | | | | | | | | | | | | | | | | | 34 | | | | | |
| | | | | | | | | | | | | | | | | | | | | | | | | | 35 | | | | | |
| | | | | | | | | | | | | | | | | | | | | | | | | | 36 | | | | | |

# $\mathcal{S}$ubject_______________________

| Week | Week____ | | | | | Week____ | | | | | Week____ | | | | | Week____ | | | | | Week____ | | | | |
|---|---|---|---|---|---|---|---|---|---|---|---|---|---|---|---|---|---|---|---|---|---|---|---|---|---|
| Day | M | T | W | T | F | M | T | W | T | F | M | T | W | T | F | M | T | W | T | F | M | T | W | T | F |
| Date | | | | | | | | | | | | | | | | | | | | | | | | | |
| *Assignments or Attendance* | | | | | | | | | | | | | | | | | | | | | | | | | |
| Name | | | | | | | | | | | | | | | | | | | | | | | | | |
| 1 | | | | | | | | | | | | | | | | | | | | | | | | | |
| 2 | | | | | | | | | | | | | | | | | | | | | | | | | |
| 3 | | | | | | | | | | | | | | | | | | | | | | | | | |
| 4 | | | | | | | | | | | | | | | | | | | | | | | | | |
| 5 | | | | | | | | | | | | | | | | | | | | | | | | | |
| 6 | | | | | | | | | | | | | | | | | | | | | | | | | |
| 7 | | | | | | | | | | | | | | | | | | | | | | | | | |
| 8 | | | | | | | | | | | | | | | | | | | | | | | | | |
| 9 | | | | | | | | | | | | | | | | | | | | | | | | | |
| 10 | | | | | | | | | | | | | | | | | | | | | | | | | |
| 11 | | | | | | | | | | | | | | | | | | | | | | | | | |
| 12 | | | | | | | | | | | | | | | | | | | | | | | | | |
| 13 | | | | | | | | | | | | | | | | | | | | | | | | | |
| 14 | | | | | | | | | | | | | | | | | | | | | | | | | |
| 15 | | | | | | | | | | | | | | | | | | | | | | | | | |
| 16 | | | | | | | | | | | | | | | | | | | | | | | | | |
| 17 | | | | | | | | | | | | | | | | | | | | | | | | | |
| 18 | | | | | | | | | | | | | | | | | | | | | | | | | |
| 19 | | | | | | | | | | | | | | | | | | | | | | | | | |
| 20 | | | | | | | | | | | | | | | | | | | | | | | | | |
| 21 | | | | | | | | | | | | | | | | | | | | | | | | | |
| 22 | | | | | | | | | | | | | | | | | | | | | | | | | |
| 23 | | | | | | | | | | | | | | | | | | | | | | | | | |
| 24 | | | | | | | | | | | | | | | | | | | | | | | | | |
| 25 | | | | | | | | | | | | | | | | | | | | | | | | | |
| 26 | | | | | | | | | | | | | | | | | | | | | | | | | |
| 27 | | | | | | | | | | | | | | | | | | | | | | | | | |
| 28 | | | | | | | | | | | | | | | | | | | | | | | | | |
| 29 | | | | | | | | | | | | | | | | | | | | | | | | | |
| 30 | | | | | | | | | | | | | | | | | | | | | | | | | |
| 31 | | | | | | | | | | | | | | | | | | | | | | | | | |
| 32 | | | | | | | | | | | | | | | | | | | | | | | | | |
| 33 | | | | | | | | | | | | | | | | | | | | | | | | | |
| 34 | | | | | | | | | | | | | | | | | | | | | | | | | |
| 35 | | | | | | | | | | | | | | | | | | | | | | | | | |
| 36 | | | | | | | | | | | | | | | | | | | | | | | | | |

# $\mathcal{P}$eriod________________________

| Week____ | | | | | Week____ | | | | | Week____ | | | | | Week____ | | | | | Week____ | | | | | | *Days Present* | *Days Absent* | *Tardies* | *Quarter Grade* | |
|---|---|---|---|---|---|---|---|---|---|---|---|---|---|---|---|---|---|---|---|---|---|---|---|---|---|---|---|---|---|---|
| M | T | W | T | F | M | T | W | T | F | M | T | W | T | F | M | T | W | T | F | M | T | W | T | F | | | | | | |
| | | | | | | | | | | | | | | | | | | | | | | | | | | | | | | |
| | | | | | | | | | | | | | | | | | | | | | | | | | | | | | | |
| | | | | | | | | | | | | | | | | | | | | | | | | | 1 | | | | | |
| | | | | | | | | | | | | | | | | | | | | | | | | | 2 | | | | | |
| | | | | | | | | | | | | | | | | | | | | | | | | | 3 | | | | | |
| | | | | | | | | | | | | | | | | | | | | | | | | | 4 | | | | | |
| | | | | | | | | | | | | | | | | | | | | | | | | | 5 | | | | | |
| | | | | | | | | | | | | | | | | | | | | | | | | | 6 | | | | | |
| | | | | | | | | | | | | | | | | | | | | | | | | | 7 | | | | | |
| | | | | | | | | | | | | | | | | | | | | | | | | | 8 | | | | | |
| | | | | | | | | | | | | | | | | | | | | | | | | | 9 | | | | | |
| | | | | | | | | | | | | | | | | | | | | | | | | | 10 | | | | | |
| | | | | | | | | | | | | | | | | | | | | | | | | | 11 | | | | | |
| | | | | | | | | | | | | | | | | | | | | | | | | | 12 | | | | | |
| | | | | | | | | | | | | | | | | | | | | | | | | | 13 | | | | | |
| | | | | | | | | | | | | | | | | | | | | | | | | | 14 | | | | | |
| | | | | | | | | | | | | | | | | | | | | | | | | | 15 | | | | | |
| | | | | | | | | | | | | | | | | | | | | | | | | | 16 | | | | | |
| | | | | | | | | | | | | | | | | | | | | | | | | | 17 | | | | | |
| | | | | | | | | | | | | | | | | | | | | | | | | | 18 | | | | | |
| | | | | | | | | | | | | | | | | | | | | | | | | | 19 | | | | | |
| | | | | | | | | | | | | | | | | | | | | | | | | | 20 | | | | | |
| | | | | | | | | | | | | | | | | | | | | | | | | | 21 | | | | | |
| | | | | | | | | | | | | | | | | | | | | | | | | | 22 | | | | | |
| | | | | | | | | | | | | | | | | | | | | | | | | | 23 | | | | | |
| | | | | | | | | | | | | | | | | | | | | | | | | | 24 | | | | | |
| | | | | | | | | | | | | | | | | | | | | | | | | | 25 | | | | | |
| | | | | | | | | | | | | | | | | | | | | | | | | | 26 | | | | | |
| | | | | | | | | | | | | | | | | | | | | | | | | | 27 | | | | | |
| | | | | | | | | | | | | | | | | | | | | | | | | | 28 | | | | | |
| | | | | | | | | | | | | | | | | | | | | | | | | | 29 | | | | | |
| | | | | | | | | | | | | | | | | | | | | | | | | | 30 | | | | | |
| | | | | | | | | | | | | | | | | | | | | | | | | | 31 | | | | | |
| | | | | | | | | | | | | | | | | | | | | | | | | | 32 | | | | | |
| | | | | | | | | | | | | | | | | | | | | | | | | | 33 | | | | | |
| | | | | | | | | | | | | | | | | | | | | | | | | | 34 | | | | | |
| | | | | | | | | | | | | | | | | | | | | | | | | | 35 | | | | | |
| | | | | | | | | | | | | | | | | | | | | | | | | | 36 | | | | | |

# $S$ubject______________________

| Week | Week____ | | | | | Week____ | | | | | Week____ | | | | | Week____ | | | | | Week____ | | | | | Week____ | | | | |
|---|---|---|---|---|---|---|---|---|---|---|---|---|---|---|---|---|---|---|---|---|---|---|---|---|---|---|
| Day | M | T | W | T | F | M | T | W | T | F | M | T | W | T | F | M | T | W | T | F | M | T | W | T | F | M | T | W | T | F |
| Date | | | | | | | | | | | | | | | | | | | | | | | | | | | | | | |
| Assignments or Attendance | | | | | | | | | | | | | | | | | | | | | | | | | | | | | | |
| Name | | | | | | | | | | | | | | | | | | | | | | | | | | | | | | |
| 1 | | | | | | | | | | | | | | | | | | | | | | | | | | | | | | |
| 2 | | | | | | | | | | | | | | | | | | | | | | | | | | | | | | |
| 3 | | | | | | | | | | | | | | | | | | | | | | | | | | | | | | |
| 4 | | | | | | | | | | | | | | | | | | | | | | | | | | | | | | |
| 5 | | | | | | | | | | | | | | | | | | | | | | | | | | | | | | |
| 6 | | | | | | | | | | | | | | | | | | | | | | | | | | | | | | |
| 7 | | | | | | | | | | | | | | | | | | | | | | | | | | | | | | |
| 8 | | | | | | | | | | | | | | | | | | | | | | | | | | | | | | |
| 9 | | | | | | | | | | | | | | | | | | | | | | | | | | | | | | |
| 10 | | | | | | | | | | | | | | | | | | | | | | | | | | | | | | |
| 11 | | | | | | | | | | | | | | | | | | | | | | | | | | | | | | |
| 12 | | | | | | | | | | | | | | | | | | | | | | | | | | | | | | |
| 13 | | | | | | | | | | | | | | | | | | | | | | | | | | | | | | |
| 14 | | | | | | | | | | | | | | | | | | | | | | | | | | | | | | |
| 15 | | | | | | | | | | | | | | | | | | | | | | | | | | | | | | |
| 16 | | | | | | | | | | | | | | | | | | | | | | | | | | | | | | |
| 17 | | | | | | | | | | | | | | | | | | | | | | | | | | | | | | |
| 18 | | | | | | | | | | | | | | | | | | | | | | | | | | | | | | |
| 19 | | | | | | | | | | | | | | | | | | | | | | | | | | | | | | |
| 20 | | | | | | | | | | | | | | | | | | | | | | | | | | | | | | |
| 21 | | | | | | | | | | | | | | | | | | | | | | | | | | | | | | |
| 22 | | | | | | | | | | | | | | | | | | | | | | | | | | | | | | |
| 23 | | | | | | | | | | | | | | | | | | | | | | | | | | | | | | |
| 24 | | | | | | | | | | | | | | | | | | | | | | | | | | | | | | |
| 25 | | | | | | | | | | | | | | | | | | | | | | | | | | | | | | |
| 26 | | | | | | | | | | | | | | | | | | | | | | | | | | | | | | |
| 27 | | | | | | | | | | | | | | | | | | | | | | | | | | | | | | |
| 28 | | | | | | | | | | | | | | | | | | | | | | | | | | | | | | |
| 29 | | | | | | | | | | | | | | | | | | | | | | | | | | | | | | |
| 30 | | | | | | | | | | | | | | | | | | | | | | | | | | | | | | |
| 31 | | | | | | | | | | | | | | | | | | | | | | | | | | | | | | |
| 32 | | | | | | | | | | | | | | | | | | | | | | | | | | | | | | |
| 33 | | | | | | | | | | | | | | | | | | | | | | | | | | | | | | |
| 34 | | | | | | | | | | | | | | | | | | | | | | | | | | | | | | |
| 35 | | | | | | | | | | | | | | | | | | | | | | | | | | | | | | |
| 36 | | | | | | | | | | | | | | | | | | | | | | | | | | | | | | |

| Week____ | | | | | Week____ | | | | | Week____ | | | | | Week____ | | | | | Week____ | | | | | | Days Present | Days Absent | Tardies | Quarter Grade | |
|---|---|---|---|---|---|---|---|---|---|---|---|---|---|---|---|---|---|---|---|---|---|---|---|---|---|---|---|---|---|---|---|
| M | T | W | T | F | M | T | W | T | F | M | T | W | T | F | M | T | W | T | F | M | T | W | T | F | | | | | | |
| | | | | | | | | | | | | | | | | | | | | | | | | | | | | | | |
| | | | | | | | | | | | | | | | | | | | | | | | | | | | | | | |
| | | | | | | | | | | | | | | | | | | | | | | | | | 1 | | | | | |
| | | | | | | | | | | | | | | | | | | | | | | | | | 2 | | | | | |
| | | | | | | | | | | | | | | | | | | | | | | | | | 3 | | | | | |
| | | | | | | | | | | | | | | | | | | | | | | | | | 4 | | | | | |
| | | | | | | | | | | | | | | | | | | | | | | | | | 5 | | | | | |
| | | | | | | | | | | | | | | | | | | | | | | | | | 6 | | | | | |
| | | | | | | | | | | | | | | | | | | | | | | | | | 7 | | | | | |
| | | | | | | | | | | | | | | | | | | | | | | | | | 8 | | | | | |
| | | | | | | | | | | | | | | | | | | | | | | | | | 9 | | | | | |
| | | | | | | | | | | | | | | | | | | | | | | | | | 10 | | | | | |
| | | | | | | | | | | | | | | | | | | | | | | | | | 11 | | | | | |
| | | | | | | | | | | | | | | | | | | | | | | | | | 12 | | | | | |
| | | | | | | | | | | | | | | | | | | | | | | | | | 13 | | | | | |
| | | | | | | | | | | | | | | | | | | | | | | | | | 14 | | | | | |
| | | | | | | | | | | | | | | | | | | | | | | | | | 15 | | | | | |
| | | | | | | | | | | | | | | | | | | | | | | | | | 16 | | | | | |
| | | | | | | | | | | | | | | | | | | | | | | | | | 17 | | | | | |
| | | | | | | | | | | | | | | | | | | | | | | | | | 18 | | | | | |
| | | | | | | | | | | | | | | | | | | | | | | | | | 19 | | | | | |
| | | | | | | | | | | | | | | | | | | | | | | | | | 20 | | | | | |
| | | | | | | | | | | | | | | | | | | | | | | | | | 21 | | | | | |
| | | | | | | | | | | | | | | | | | | | | | | | | | 22 | | | | | |
| | | | | | | | | | | | | | | | | | | | | | | | | | 23 | | | | | |
| | | | | | | | | | | | | | | | | | | | | | | | | | 24 | | | | | |
| | | | | | | | | | | | | | | | | | | | | | | | | | 25 | | | | | |
| | | | | | | | | | | | | | | | | | | | | | | | | | 26 | | | | | |
| | | | | | | | | | | | | | | | | | | | | | | | | | 27 | | | | | |
| | | | | | | | | | | | | | | | | | | | | | | | | | 28 | | | | | |
| | | | | | | | | | | | | | | | | | | | | | | | | | 29 | | | | | |
| | | | | | | | | | | | | | | | | | | | | | | | | | 30 | | | | | |
| | | | | | | | | | | | | | | | | | | | | | | | | | 31 | | | | | |
| | | | | | | | | | | | | | | | | | | | | | | | | | 32 | | | | | |
| | | | | | | | | | | | | | | | | | | | | | | | | | 33 | | | | | |
| | | | | | | | | | | | | | | | | | | | | | | | | | 34 | | | | | |
| | | | | | | | | | | | | | | | | | | | | | | | | | 35 | | | | | |
| | | | | | | | | | | | | | | | | | | | | | | | | | 36 | | | | | |

# $\mathcal{S}ubject$ ______________________________

| Week | Week____ | | | | | Week____ | | | | | Week____ | | | | | Week____ | | | | | Week____ | | | | | Week____ | | | | |
|---|---|---|---|---|---|---|---|---|---|---|---|---|---|---|---|---|---|---|---|---|---|---|---|---|---|---|---|---|---|---|
| Day | M | T | W | T | F | M | T | W | T | F | M | T | W | T | F | M | T | W | T | F | M | T | W | T | F | M | T | W | T | F |
| Date | | | | | | | | | | | | | | | | | | | | | | | | | | | | | | |
| Assignments or Attendance | | | | | | | | | | | | | | | | | | | | | | | | | | | | | | |
| Name | | | | | | | | | | | | | | | | | | | | | | | | | | | | | | |
| 1 | | | | | | | | | | | | | | | | | | | | | | | | | | | | | | |
| 2 | | | | | | | | | | | | | | | | | | | | | | | | | | | | | | |
| 3 | | | | | | | | | | | | | | | | | | | | | | | | | | | | | | |
| 4 | | | | | | | | | | | | | | | | | | | | | | | | | | | | | | |
| 5 | | | | | | | | | | | | | | | | | | | | | | | | | | | | | | |
| 6 | | | | | | | | | | | | | | | | | | | | | | | | | | | | | | |
| 7 | | | | | | | | | | | | | | | | | | | | | | | | | | | | | | |
| 8 | | | | | | | | | | | | | | | | | | | | | | | | | | | | | | |
| 9 | | | | | | | | | | | | | | | | | | | | | | | | | | | | | | |
| 10 | | | | | | | | | | | | | | | | | | | | | | | | | | | | | | |
| 11 | | | | | | | | | | | | | | | | | | | | | | | | | | | | | | |
| 12 | | | | | | | | | | | | | | | | | | | | | | | | | | | | | | |
| 13 | | | | | | | | | | | | | | | | | | | | | | | | | | | | | | |
| 14 | | | | | | | | | | | | | | | | | | | | | | | | | | | | | | |
| 15 | | | | | | | | | | | | | | | | | | | | | | | | | | | | | | |
| 16 | | | | | | | | | | | | | | | | | | | | | | | | | | | | | | |
| 17 | | | | | | | | | | | | | | | | | | | | | | | | | | | | | | |
| 18 | | | | | | | | | | | | | | | | | | | | | | | | | | | | | | |
| 19 | | | | | | | | | | | | | | | | | | | | | | | | | | | | | | |
| 20 | | | | | | | | | | | | | | | | | | | | | | | | | | | | | | |
| 21 | | | | | | | | | | | | | | | | | | | | | | | | | | | | | | |
| 22 | | | | | | | | | | | | | | | | | | | | | | | | | | | | | | |
| 23 | | | | | | | | | | | | | | | | | | | | | | | | | | | | | | |
| 24 | | | | | | | | | | | | | | | | | | | | | | | | | | | | | | |
| 25 | | | | | | | | | | | | | | | | | | | | | | | | | | | | | | |
| 26 | | | | | | | | | | | | | | | | | | | | | | | | | | | | | | |
| 27 | | | | | | | | | | | | | | | | | | | | | | | | | | | | | | |
| 28 | | | | | | | | | | | | | | | | | | | | | | | | | | | | | | |
| 29 | | | | | | | | | | | | | | | | | | | | | | | | | | | | | | |
| 30 | | | | | | | | | | | | | | | | | | | | | | | | | | | | | | |
| 31 | | | | | | | | | | | | | | | | | | | | | | | | | | | | | | |
| 32 | | | | | | | | | | | | | | | | | | | | | | | | | | | | | | |
| 33 | | | | | | | | | | | | | | | | | | | | | | | | | | | | | | |
| 34 | | | | | | | | | | | | | | | | | | | | | | | | | | | | | | |
| 35 | | | | | | | | | | | | | | | | | | | | | | | | | | | | | | |
| 36 | | | | | | | | | | | | | | | | | | | | | | | | | | | | | | |

# Period________________________

| Week____ | | | | | Week____ | | | | | Week____ | | | | | Week____ | | | | | Week____ | | | | | | Days Present | Days Absent | Tardies | Quarter Grade | | |
|---|---|---|---|---|---|---|---|---|---|---|---|---|---|---|---|---|---|---|---|---|---|---|---|---|---|---|---|---|---|---|
| M | T | W | T | F | M | T | W | T | F | M | T | W | T | F | M | T | W | T | F | M | T | W | T | F | | | | | | | |
| | | | | | | | | | | | | | | | | | | | | | | | | | 1 | | | | | | |
| | | | | | | | | | | | | | | | | | | | | | | | | | 2 | | | | | | |
| | | | | | | | | | | | | | | | | | | | | | | | | | 3 | | | | | | |
| | | | | | | | | | | | | | | | | | | | | | | | | | 4 | | | | | | |
| | | | | | | | | | | | | | | | | | | | | | | | | | 5 | | | | | | |
| | | | | | | | | | | | | | | | | | | | | | | | | | 6 | | | | | | |
| | | | | | | | | | | | | | | | | | | | | | | | | | 7 | | | | | | |
| | | | | | | | | | | | | | | | | | | | | | | | | | 8 | | | | | | |
| | | | | | | | | | | | | | | | | | | | | | | | | | 9 | | | | | | |
| | | | | | | | | | | | | | | | | | | | | | | | | | 10 | | | | | | |
| | | | | | | | | | | | | | | | | | | | | | | | | | 11 | | | | | | |
| | | | | | | | | | | | | | | | | | | | | | | | | | 12 | | | | | | |
| | | | | | | | | | | | | | | | | | | | | | | | | | 13 | | | | | | |
| | | | | | | | | | | | | | | | | | | | | | | | | | 14 | | | | | | |
| | | | | | | | | | | | | | | | | | | | | | | | | | 15 | | | | | | |
| | | | | | | | | | | | | | | | | | | | | | | | | | 16 | | | | | | |
| | | | | | | | | | | | | | | | | | | | | | | | | | 17 | | | | | | |
| | | | | | | | | | | | | | | | | | | | | | | | | | 18 | | | | | | |
| | | | | | | | | | | | | | | | | | | | | | | | | | 19 | | | | | | |
| | | | | | | | | | | | | | | | | | | | | | | | | | 20 | | | | | | |
| | | | | | | | | | | | | | | | | | | | | | | | | | 21 | | | | | | |
| | | | | | | | | | | | | | | | | | | | | | | | | | 22 | | | | | | |
| | | | | | | | | | | | | | | | | | | | | | | | | | 23 | | | | | | |
| | | | | | | | | | | | | | | | | | | | | | | | | | 24 | | | | | | |
| | | | | | | | | | | | | | | | | | | | | | | | | | 25 | | | | | | |
| | | | | | | | | | | | | | | | | | | | | | | | | | 26 | | | | | | |
| | | | | | | | | | | | | | | | | | | | | | | | | | 27 | | | | | | |
| | | | | | | | | | | | | | | | | | | | | | | | | | 28 | | | | | | |
| | | | | | | | | | | | | | | | | | | | | | | | | | 29 | | | | | | |
| | | | | | | | | | | | | | | | | | | | | | | | | | 30 | | | | | | |
| | | | | | | | | | | | | | | | | | | | | | | | | | 31 | | | | | | |
| | | | | | | | | | | | | | | | | | | | | | | | | | 32 | | | | | | |
| | | | | | | | | | | | | | | | | | | | | | | | | | 33 | | | | | | |
| | | | | | | | | | | | | | | | | | | | | | | | | | 34 | | | | | | |
| | | | | | | | | | | | | | | | | | | | | | | | | | 35 | | | | | | |
| | | | | | | | | | | | | | | | | | | | | | | | | | 36 | | | | | | |

# $\mathcal{S}$ubject __________________________

| Week | Week____ | | | | | Week____ | | | | | Week____ | | | | | Week____ | | | | | Week____ | | | | |
|---|---|---|---|---|---|---|---|---|---|---|---|---|---|---|---|---|---|---|---|---|---|---|---|---|---|
| Day | M | T | W | T | F | M | T | W | T | F | M | T | W | T | F | M | T | W | T | F | M | T | W | T | F |
| Date | | | | | | | | | | | | | | | | | | | | | | | | | |
| Assignments or Attendance | | | | | | | | | | | | | | | | | | | | | | | | | |
| Name | | | | | | | | | | | | | | | | | | | | | | | | | |
| 1 | | | | | | | | | | | | | | | | | | | | | | | | | |
| 2 | | | | | | | | | | | | | | | | | | | | | | | | | |
| 3 | | | | | | | | | | | | | | | | | | | | | | | | | |
| 4 | | | | | | | | | | | | | | | | | | | | | | | | | |
| 5 | | | | | | | | | | | | | | | | | | | | | | | | | |
| 6 | | | | | | | | | | | | | | | | | | | | | | | | | |
| 7 | | | | | | | | | | | | | | | | | | | | | | | | | |
| 8 | | | | | | | | | | | | | | | | | | | | | | | | | |
| 9 | | | | | | | | | | | | | | | | | | | | | | | | | |
| 10 | | | | | | | | | | | | | | | | | | | | | | | | | |
| 11 | | | | | | | | | | | | | | | | | | | | | | | | | |
| 12 | | | | | | | | | | | | | | | | | | | | | | | | | |
| 13 | | | | | | | | | | | | | | | | | | | | | | | | | |
| 14 | | | | | | | | | | | | | | | | | | | | | | | | | |
| 15 | | | | | | | | | | | | | | | | | | | | | | | | | |
| 16 | | | | | | | | | | | | | | | | | | | | | | | | | |
| 17 | | | | | | | | | | | | | | | | | | | | | | | | | |
| 18 | | | | | | | | | | | | | | | | | | | | | | | | | |
| 19 | | | | | | | | | | | | | | | | | | | | | | | | | |
| 20 | | | | | | | | | | | | | | | | | | | | | | | | | |
| 21 | | | | | | | | | | | | | | | | | | | | | | | | | |
| 22 | | | | | | | | | | | | | | | | | | | | | | | | | |
| 23 | | | | | | | | | | | | | | | | | | | | | | | | | |
| 24 | | | | | | | | | | | | | | | | | | | | | | | | | |
| 25 | | | | | | | | | | | | | | | | | | | | | | | | | |
| 26 | | | | | | | | | | | | | | | | | | | | | | | | | |
| 27 | | | | | | | | | | | | | | | | | | | | | | | | | |
| 28 | | | | | | | | | | | | | | | | | | | | | | | | | |
| 29 | | | | | | | | | | | | | | | | | | | | | | | | | |
| 30 | | | | | | | | | | | | | | | | | | | | | | | | | |
| 31 | | | | | | | | | | | | | | | | | | | | | | | | | |
| 32 | | | | | | | | | | | | | | | | | | | | | | | | | |
| 33 | | | | | | | | | | | | | | | | | | | | | | | | | |
| 34 | | | | | | | | | | | | | | | | | | | | | | | | | |
| 35 | | | | | | | | | | | | | | | | | | | | | | | | | |
| 36 | | | | | | | | | | | | | | | | | | | | | | | | | |

# *Period*_______________________

| Week____ | | | | | Week____ | | | | | Week____ | | | | | Week____ | | | | | Week____ | | | | | | *Days Present* | *Days Absent* | *Tardies* | *Quarter Grade* | |
|---|---|---|---|---|---|---|---|---|---|---|---|---|---|---|---|---|---|---|---|---|---|---|---|---|---|---|---|---|---|
| M | T | W | T | F | M | T | W | T | F | M | T | W | T | F | M | T | W | T | F | M | T | W | T | F | | | | | | |
| | | | | | | | | | | | | | | | | | | | | | | | | | | | | | | |
| | | | | | | | | | | | | | | | | | | | | | | | | | | | | | | |
| | | | | | | | | | | | | | | | | | | | | | | | | | 1 | | | | | |
| | | | | | | | | | | | | | | | | | | | | | | | | | 2 | | | | | |
| | | | | | | | | | | | | | | | | | | | | | | | | | 3 | | | | | |
| | | | | | | | | | | | | | | | | | | | | | | | | | 4 | | | | | |
| | | | | | | | | | | | | | | | | | | | | | | | | | 5 | | | | | |
| | | | | | | | | | | | | | | | | | | | | | | | | | 6 | | | | | |
| | | | | | | | | | | | | | | | | | | | | | | | | | 7 | | | | | |
| | | | | | | | | | | | | | | | | | | | | | | | | | 8 | | | | | |
| | | | | | | | | | | | | | | | | | | | | | | | | | 9 | | | | | |
| | | | | | | | | | | | | | | | | | | | | | | | | | 10 | | | | | |
| | | | | | | | | | | | | | | | | | | | | | | | | | 11 | | | | | |
| | | | | | | | | | | | | | | | | | | | | | | | | | 12 | | | | | |
| | | | | | | | | | | | | | | | | | | | | | | | | | 13 | | | | | |
| | | | | | | | | | | | | | | | | | | | | | | | | | 14 | | | | | |
| | | | | | | | | | | | | | | | | | | | | | | | | | 15 | | | | | |
| | | | | | | | | | | | | | | | | | | | | | | | | | 16 | | | | | |
| | | | | | | | | | | | | | | | | | | | | | | | | | 17 | | | | | |
| | | | | | | | | | | | | | | | | | | | | | | | | | 18 | | | | | |
| | | | | | | | | | | | | | | | | | | | | | | | | | 19 | | | | | |
| | | | | | | | | | | | | | | | | | | | | | | | | | 20 | | | | | |
| | | | | | | | | | | | | | | | | | | | | | | | | | 21 | | | | | |
| | | | | | | | | | | | | | | | | | | | | | | | | | 22 | | | | | |
| | | | | | | | | | | | | | | | | | | | | | | | | | 23 | | | | | |
| | | | | | | | | | | | | | | | | | | | | | | | | | 24 | | | | | |
| | | | | | | | | | | | | | | | | | | | | | | | | | 25 | | | | | |
| | | | | | | | | | | | | | | | | | | | | | | | | | 26 | | | | | |
| | | | | | | | | | | | | | | | | | | | | | | | | | 27 | | | | | |
| | | | | | | | | | | | | | | | | | | | | | | | | | 28 | | | | | |
| | | | | | | | | | | | | | | | | | | | | | | | | | 29 | | | | | |
| | | | | | | | | | | | | | | | | | | | | | | | | | 30 | | | | | |
| | | | | | | | | | | | | | | | | | | | | | | | | | 31 | | | | | |
| | | | | | | | | | | | | | | | | | | | | | | | | | 32 | | | | | |
| | | | | | | | | | | | | | | | | | | | | | | | | | 33 | | | | | |
| | | | | | | | | | | | | | | | | | | | | | | | | | 34 | | | | | |
| | | | | | | | | | | | | | | | | | | | | | | | | | 35 | | | | | |
| | | | | | | | | | | | | | | | | | | | | | | | | | 36 | | | | | |

# Subject_____________________

| Week | Week____ | | | | | Week____ | | | | | Week____ | | | | | Week____ | | | | | Week____ | | | | |
|---|---|---|---|---|---|---|---|---|---|---|---|---|---|---|---|---|---|---|---|---|---|---|---|---|---|
| Day | M | T | W | T | F | M | T | W | T | F | M | T | W | T | F | M | T | W | T | F | M | T | W | T | F |
| Date | | | | | | | | | | | | | | | | | | | | | | | | | |
| Assignments or Attendance | | | | | | | | | | | | | | | | | | | | | | | | | |
| Name | | | | | | | | | | | | | | | | | | | | | | | | | |
| 1 | | | | | | | | | | | | | | | | | | | | | | | | | |
| 2 | | | | | | | | | | | | | | | | | | | | | | | | | |
| 3 | | | | | | | | | | | | | | | | | | | | | | | | | |
| 4 | | | | | | | | | | | | | | | | | | | | | | | | | |
| 5 | | | | | | | | | | | | | | | | | | | | | | | | | |
| 6 | | | | | | | | | | | | | | | | | | | | | | | | | |
| 7 | | | | | | | | | | | | | | | | | | | | | | | | | |
| 8 | | | | | | | | | | | | | | | | | | | | | | | | | |
| 9 | | | | | | | | | | | | | | | | | | | | | | | | | |
| 10 | | | | | | | | | | | | | | | | | | | | | | | | | |
| 11 | | | | | | | | | | | | | | | | | | | | | | | | | |
| 12 | | | | | | | | | | | | | | | | | | | | | | | | | |
| 13 | | | | | | | | | | | | | | | | | | | | | | | | | |
| 14 | | | | | | | | | | | | | | | | | | | | | | | | | |
| 15 | | | | | | | | | | | | | | | | | | | | | | | | | |
| 16 | | | | | | | | | | | | | | | | | | | | | | | | | |
| 17 | | | | | | | | | | | | | | | | | | | | | | | | | |
| 18 | | | | | | | | | | | | | | | | | | | | | | | | | |
| 19 | | | | | | | | | | | | | | | | | | | | | | | | | |
| 20 | | | | | | | | | | | | | | | | | | | | | | | | | |
| 21 | | | | | | | | | | | | | | | | | | | | | | | | | |
| 22 | | | | | | | | | | | | | | | | | | | | | | | | | |
| 23 | | | | | | | | | | | | | | | | | | | | | | | | | |
| 24 | | | | | | | | | | | | | | | | | | | | | | | | | |
| 25 | | | | | | | | | | | | | | | | | | | | | | | | | |
| 26 | | | | | | | | | | | | | | | | | | | | | | | | | |
| 27 | | | | | | | | | | | | | | | | | | | | | | | | | |
| 28 | | | | | | | | | | | | | | | | | | | | | | | | | |
| 29 | | | | | | | | | | | | | | | | | | | | | | | | | |
| 30 | | | | | | | | | | | | | | | | | | | | | | | | | |
| 31 | | | | | | | | | | | | | | | | | | | | | | | | | |
| 32 | | | | | | | | | | | | | | | | | | | | | | | | | |
| 33 | | | | | | | | | | | | | | | | | | | | | | | | | |
| 34 | | | | | | | | | | | | | | | | | | | | | | | | | |
| 35 | | | | | | | | | | | | | | | | | | | | | | | | | |
| 36 | | | | | | | | | | | | | | | | | | | | | | | | | |

# *Period*_______________________

| Week____ | | | | | Week____ | | | | | Week____ | | | | | Week____ | | | | | Week____ | | | | | | Days Present | Days Absent | Tardies | Quarter Grade | |
|---|---|---|---|---|---|---|---|---|---|---|---|---|---|---|---|---|---|---|---|---|---|---|---|---|---|---|---|---|---|
| M | T | W | T | F | M | T | W | T | F | M | T | W | T | F | M | T | W | T | F | M | T | W | T | F | | | | | | |
| | | | | | | | | | | | | | | | | | | | | | | | | | | | | | | |
| | | | | | | | | | | | | | | | | | | | | | | | | | | | | | | |
| | | | | | | | | | | | | | | | | | | | | | | | | | 1 | | | | | |
| | | | | | | | | | | | | | | | | | | | | | | | | | 2 | | | | | |
| | | | | | | | | | | | | | | | | | | | | | | | | | 3 | | | | | |
| | | | | | | | | | | | | | | | | | | | | | | | | | 4 | | | | | |
| | | | | | | | | | | | | | | | | | | | | | | | | | 5 | | | | | |
| | | | | | | | | | | | | | | | | | | | | | | | | | 6 | | | | | |
| | | | | | | | | | | | | | | | | | | | | | | | | | 7 | | | | | |
| | | | | | | | | | | | | | | | | | | | | | | | | | 8 | | | | | |
| | | | | | | | | | | | | | | | | | | | | | | | | | 9 | | | | | |
| | | | | | | | | | | | | | | | | | | | | | | | | | 10 | | | | | |
| | | | | | | | | | | | | | | | | | | | | | | | | | 11 | | | | | |
| | | | | | | | | | | | | | | | | | | | | | | | | | 12 | | | | | |
| | | | | | | | | | | | | | | | | | | | | | | | | | 13 | | | | | |
| | | | | | | | | | | | | | | | | | | | | | | | | | 14 | | | | | |
| | | | | | | | | | | | | | | | | | | | | | | | | | 15 | | | | | |
| | | | | | | | | | | | | | | | | | | | | | | | | | 16 | | | | | |
| | | | | | | | | | | | | | | | | | | | | | | | | | 17 | | | | | |
| | | | | | | | | | | | | | | | | | | | | | | | | | 18 | | | | | |
| | | | | | | | | | | | | | | | | | | | | | | | | | 19 | | | | | |
| | | | | | | | | | | | | | | | | | | | | | | | | | 20 | | | | | |
| | | | | | | | | | | | | | | | | | | | | | | | | | 21 | | | | | |
| | | | | | | | | | | | | | | | | | | | | | | | | | 22 | | | | | |
| | | | | | | | | | | | | | | | | | | | | | | | | | 23 | | | | | |
| | | | | | | | | | | | | | | | | | | | | | | | | | 24 | | | | | |
| | | | | | | | | | | | | | | | | | | | | | | | | | 25 | | | | | |
| | | | | | | | | | | | | | | | | | | | | | | | | | 26 | | | | | |
| | | | | | | | | | | | | | | | | | | | | | | | | | 27 | | | | | |
| | | | | | | | | | | | | | | | | | | | | | | | | | 28 | | | | | |
| | | | | | | | | | | | | | | | | | | | | | | | | | 29 | | | | | |
| | | | | | | | | | | | | | | | | | | | | | | | | | 30 | | | | | |
| | | | | | | | | | | | | | | | | | | | | | | | | | 31 | | | | | |
| | | | | | | | | | | | | | | | | | | | | | | | | | 32 | | | | | |
| | | | | | | | | | | | | | | | | | | | | | | | | | 33 | | | | | |
| | | | | | | | | | | | | | | | | | | | | | | | | | 34 | | | | | |
| | | | | | | | | | | | | | | | | | | | | | | | | | 35 | | | | | |
| | | | | | | | | | | | | | | | | | | | | | | | | | 36 | | | | | |

# $\mathcal{S}$ubject________________________

| Week | Week____ | | | | | Week____ | | | | | Week____ | | | | | Week____ | | | | | Week____ | | | | | Week____ | | | | |
|---|---|---|---|---|---|---|---|---|---|---|---|---|---|---|---|---|---|---|---|---|---|---|---|---|---|
| Day | M | T | W | T | F | M | T | W | T | F | M | T | W | T | F | M | T | W | T | F | M | T | W | T | F |
| Date | | | | | | | | | | | | | | | | | | | | | | | | | |
| Assignments or Attendance | | | | | | | | | | | | | | | | | | | | | | | | | |
| Name | | | | | | | | | | | | | | | | | | | | | | | | | |
| 1 | | | | | | | | | | | | | | | | | | | | | | | | | |
| 2 | | | | | | | | | | | | | | | | | | | | | | | | | |
| 3 | | | | | | | | | | | | | | | | | | | | | | | | | |
| 4 | | | | | | | | | | | | | | | | | | | | | | | | | |
| 5 | | | | | | | | | | | | | | | | | | | | | | | | | |
| 6 | | | | | | | | | | | | | | | | | | | | | | | | | |
| 7 | | | | | | | | | | | | | | | | | | | | | | | | | |
| 8 | | | | | | | | | | | | | | | | | | | | | | | | | |
| 9 | | | | | | | | | | | | | | | | | | | | | | | | | |
| 10 | | | | | | | | | | | | | | | | | | | | | | | | | |
| 11 | | | | | | | | | | | | | | | | | | | | | | | | | |
| 12 | | | | | | | | | | | | | | | | | | | | | | | | | |
| 13 | | | | | | | | | | | | | | | | | | | | | | | | | |
| 14 | | | | | | | | | | | | | | | | | | | | | | | | | |
| 15 | | | | | | | | | | | | | | | | | | | | | | | | | |
| 16 | | | | | | | | | | | | | | | | | | | | | | | | | |
| 17 | | | | | | | | | | | | | | | | | | | | | | | | | |
| 18 | | | | | | | | | | | | | | | | | | | | | | | | | |
| 19 | | | | | | | | | | | | | | | | | | | | | | | | | |
| 20 | | | | | | | | | | | | | | | | | | | | | | | | | |
| 21 | | | | | | | | | | | | | | | | | | | | | | | | | |
| 22 | | | | | | | | | | | | | | | | | | | | | | | | | |
| 23 | | | | | | | | | | | | | | | | | | | | | | | | | |
| 24 | | | | | | | | | | | | | | | | | | | | | | | | | |
| 25 | | | | | | | | | | | | | | | | | | | | | | | | | |
| 26 | | | | | | | | | | | | | | | | | | | | | | | | | |
| 27 | | | | | | | | | | | | | | | | | | | | | | | | | |
| 28 | | | | | | | | | | | | | | | | | | | | | | | | | |
| 29 | | | | | | | | | | | | | | | | | | | | | | | | | |
| 30 | | | | | | | | | | | | | | | | | | | | | | | | | |
| 31 | | | | | | | | | | | | | | | | | | | | | | | | | |
| 32 | | | | | | | | | | | | | | | | | | | | | | | | | |
| 33 | | | | | | | | | | | | | | | | | | | | | | | | | |
| 34 | | | | | | | | | | | | | | | | | | | | | | | | | |
| 35 | | | | | | | | | | | | | | | | | | | | | | | | | |
| 36 | | | | | | | | | | | | | | | | | | | | | | | | | |

# Period _______________________________

| | Week ____ | | | | | Week ____ | | | | | Week ____ | | | | | Week ____ | | | | | Week ____ | | | | | | Days Present | Days Absent | Tardies | Quarter Grade | |
|---|---|---|---|---|---|---|---|---|---|---|---|---|---|---|---|---|---|---|---|---|---|---|---|---|---|---|---|---|---|---|---|
| | M | T | W | T | F | M | T | W | T | F | M | T | W | T | F | M | T | W | T | F | M | T | W | T | F | | | | | | |
| 1 | | | | | | | | | | | | | | | | | | | | | | | | | | | | | | | |
| 2 | | | | | | | | | | | | | | | | | | | | | | | | | | | | | | | |
| 3 | | | | | | | | | | | | | | | | | | | | | | | | | | | | | | | |
| 4 | | | | | | | | | | | | | | | | | | | | | | | | | | | | | | | |
| 5 | | | | | | | | | | | | | | | | | | | | | | | | | | | | | | | |
| 6 | | | | | | | | | | | | | | | | | | | | | | | | | | | | | | | |
| 7 | | | | | | | | | | | | | | | | | | | | | | | | | | | | | | | |
| 8 | | | | | | | | | | | | | | | | | | | | | | | | | | | | | | | |
| 9 | | | | | | | | | | | | | | | | | | | | | | | | | | | | | | | |
| 10 | | | | | | | | | | | | | | | | | | | | | | | | | | | | | | | |
| 11 | | | | | | | | | | | | | | | | | | | | | | | | | | | | | | | |
| 12 | | | | | | | | | | | | | | | | | | | | | | | | | | | | | | | |
| 13 | | | | | | | | | | | | | | | | | | | | | | | | | | | | | | | |
| 14 | | | | | | | | | | | | | | | | | | | | | | | | | | | | | | | |
| 15 | | | | | | | | | | | | | | | | | | | | | | | | | | | | | | | |
| 16 | | | | | | | | | | | | | | | | | | | | | | | | | | | | | | | |
| 17 | | | | | | | | | | | | | | | | | | | | | | | | | | | | | | | |
| 18 | | | | | | | | | | | | | | | | | | | | | | | | | | | | | | | |
| 19 | | | | | | | | | | | | | | | | | | | | | | | | | | | | | | | |
| 20 | | | | | | | | | | | | | | | | | | | | | | | | | | | | | | | |
| 21 | | | | | | | | | | | | | | | | | | | | | | | | | | | | | | | |
| 22 | | | | | | | | | | | | | | | | | | | | | | | | | | | | | | | |
| 23 | | | | | | | | | | | | | | | | | | | | | | | | | | | | | | | |
| 24 | | | | | | | | | | | | | | | | | | | | | | | | | | | | | | | |
| 25 | | | | | | | | | | | | | | | | | | | | | | | | | | | | | | | |
| 26 | | | | | | | | | | | | | | | | | | | | | | | | | | | | | | | |
| 27 | | | | | | | | | | | | | | | | | | | | | | | | | | | | | | | |
| 28 | | | | | | | | | | | | | | | | | | | | | | | | | | | | | | | |
| 29 | | | | | | | | | | | | | | | | | | | | | | | | | | | | | | | |
| 30 | | | | | | | | | | | | | | | | | | | | | | | | | | | | | | | |
| 31 | | | | | | | | | | | | | | | | | | | | | | | | | | | | | | | |
| 32 | | | | | | | | | | | | | | | | | | | | | | | | | | | | | | | |
| 33 | | | | | | | | | | | | | | | | | | | | | | | | | | | | | | | |
| 34 | | | | | | | | | | | | | | | | | | | | | | | | | | | | | | | |
| 35 | | | | | | | | | | | | | | | | | | | | | | | | | | | | | | | |
| 36 | | | | | | | | | | | | | | | | | | | | | | | | | | | | | | | |

# Subject _______________________

| Week | Week____ | | | | | Week____ | | | | | Week____ | | | | | Week____ | | | | | Week____ | | | | | Week____ | | | | |
|---|---|---|---|---|---|---|---|---|---|---|---|---|---|---|---|---|---|---|---|---|---|---|---|---|---|---|---|---|---|---|
| Day | M | T | W | T | F | M | T | W | T | F | M | T | W | T | F | M | T | W | T | F | M | T | W | T | F | M | T | W | T | F |
| Date | | | | | | | | | | | | | | | | | | | | | | | | | | | | | | |
| Assignments or Attendance | | | | | | | | | | | | | | | | | | | | | | | | | | | | | | |
| Name | | | | | | | | | | | | | | | | | | | | | | | | | | | | | | |
| 1 | | | | | | | | | | | | | | | | | | | | | | | | | | | | | | |
| 2 | | | | | | | | | | | | | | | | | | | | | | | | | | | | | | |
| 3 | | | | | | | | | | | | | | | | | | | | | | | | | | | | | | |
| 4 | | | | | | | | | | | | | | | | | | | | | | | | | | | | | | |
| 5 | | | | | | | | | | | | | | | | | | | | | | | | | | | | | | |
| 6 | | | | | | | | | | | | | | | | | | | | | | | | | | | | | | |
| 7 | | | | | | | | | | | | | | | | | | | | | | | | | | | | | | |
| 8 | | | | | | | | | | | | | | | | | | | | | | | | | | | | | | |
| 9 | | | | | | | | | | | | | | | | | | | | | | | | | | | | | | |
| 10 | | | | | | | | | | | | | | | | | | | | | | | | | | | | | | |
| 11 | | | | | | | | | | | | | | | | | | | | | | | | | | | | | | |
| 12 | | | | | | | | | | | | | | | | | | | | | | | | | | | | | | |
| 13 | | | | | | | | | | | | | | | | | | | | | | | | | | | | | | |
| 14 | | | | | | | | | | | | | | | | | | | | | | | | | | | | | | |
| 15 | | | | | | | | | | | | | | | | | | | | | | | | | | | | | | |
| 16 | | | | | | | | | | | | | | | | | | | | | | | | | | | | | | |
| 17 | | | | | | | | | | | | | | | | | | | | | | | | | | | | | | |
| 18 | | | | | | | | | | | | | | | | | | | | | | | | | | | | | | |
| 19 | | | | | | | | | | | | | | | | | | | | | | | | | | | | | | |
| 20 | | | | | | | | | | | | | | | | | | | | | | | | | | | | | | |
| 21 | | | | | | | | | | | | | | | | | | | | | | | | | | | | | | |
| 22 | | | | | | | | | | | | | | | | | | | | | | | | | | | | | | |
| 23 | | | | | | | | | | | | | | | | | | | | | | | | | | | | | | |
| 24 | | | | | | | | | | | | | | | | | | | | | | | | | | | | | | |
| 25 | | | | | | | | | | | | | | | | | | | | | | | | | | | | | | |
| 26 | | | | | | | | | | | | | | | | | | | | | | | | | | | | | | |
| 27 | | | | | | | | | | | | | | | | | | | | | | | | | | | | | | |
| 28 | | | | | | | | | | | | | | | | | | | | | | | | | | | | | | |
| 29 | | | | | | | | | | | | | | | | | | | | | | | | | | | | | | |
| 30 | | | | | | | | | | | | | | | | | | | | | | | | | | | | | | |
| 31 | | | | | | | | | | | | | | | | | | | | | | | | | | | | | | |
| 32 | | | | | | | | | | | | | | | | | | | | | | | | | | | | | | |
| 33 | | | | | | | | | | | | | | | | | | | | | | | | | | | | | | |
| 34 | | | | | | | | | | | | | | | | | | | | | | | | | | | | | | |
| 35 | | | | | | | | | | | | | | | | | | | | | | | | | | | | | | |
| 36 | | | | | | | | | | | | | | | | | | | | | | | | | | | | | | |

# *Period*_______________________

| Week____ | | | | | Week____ | | | | | Week____ | | | | | Week____ | | | | | Week____ | | | | | | Days Present | Days Absent | Tardies | Quarter Grade | |
|---|---|---|---|---|---|---|---|---|---|---|---|---|---|---|---|---|---|---|---|---|---|---|---|---|---|---|---|---|---|---|
| M | T | W | T | F | M | T | W | T | F | M | T | W | T | F | M | T | W | T | F | M | T | W | T | F | | | | | | |
| | | | | | | | | | | | | | | | | | | | | | | | | | | | | | | |
| | | | | | | | | | | | | | | | | | | | | | | | | | | | | | | |
| | | | | | | | | | | | | | | | | | | | | | | | | | 1 | | | | | |
| | | | | | | | | | | | | | | | | | | | | | | | | | 2 | | | | | |
| | | | | | | | | | | | | | | | | | | | | | | | | | 3 | | | | | |
| | | | | | | | | | | | | | | | | | | | | | | | | | 4 | | | | | |
| | | | | | | | | | | | | | | | | | | | | | | | | | 5 | | | | | |
| | | | | | | | | | | | | | | | | | | | | | | | | | 6 | | | | | |
| | | | | | | | | | | | | | | | | | | | | | | | | | 7 | | | | | |
| | | | | | | | | | | | | | | | | | | | | | | | | | 8 | | | | | |
| | | | | | | | | | | | | | | | | | | | | | | | | | 9 | | | | | |
| | | | | | | | | | | | | | | | | | | | | | | | | | 10 | | | | | |
| | | | | | | | | | | | | | | | | | | | | | | | | | 11 | | | | | |
| | | | | | | | | | | | | | | | | | | | | | | | | | 12 | | | | | |
| | | | | | | | | | | | | | | | | | | | | | | | | | 13 | | | | | |
| | | | | | | | | | | | | | | | | | | | | | | | | | 14 | | | | | |
| | | | | | | | | | | | | | | | | | | | | | | | | | 15 | | | | | |
| | | | | | | | | | | | | | | | | | | | | | | | | | 16 | | | | | |
| | | | | | | | | | | | | | | | | | | | | | | | | | 17 | | | | | |
| | | | | | | | | | | | | | | | | | | | | | | | | | 18 | | | | | |
| | | | | | | | | | | | | | | | | | | | | | | | | | 19 | | | | | |
| | | | | | | | | | | | | | | | | | | | | | | | | | 20 | | | | | |
| | | | | | | | | | | | | | | | | | | | | | | | | | 21 | | | | | |
| | | | | | | | | | | | | | | | | | | | | | | | | | 22 | | | | | |
| | | | | | | | | | | | | | | | | | | | | | | | | | 23 | | | | | |
| | | | | | | | | | | | | | | | | | | | | | | | | | 24 | | | | | |
| | | | | | | | | | | | | | | | | | | | | | | | | | 25 | | | | | |
| | | | | | | | | | | | | | | | | | | | | | | | | | 26 | | | | | |
| | | | | | | | | | | | | | | | | | | | | | | | | | 27 | | | | | |
| | | | | | | | | | | | | | | | | | | | | | | | | | 28 | | | | | |
| | | | | | | | | | | | | | | | | | | | | | | | | | 29 | | | | | |
| | | | | | | | | | | | | | | | | | | | | | | | | | 30 | | | | | |
| | | | | | | | | | | | | | | | | | | | | | | | | | 31 | | | | | |
| | | | | | | | | | | | | | | | | | | | | | | | | | 32 | | | | | |
| | | | | | | | | | | | | | | | | | | | | | | | | | 33 | | | | | |
| | | | | | | | | | | | | | | | | | | | | | | | | | 34 | | | | | |
| | | | | | | | | | | | | | | | | | | | | | | | | | 35 | | | | | |
| | | | | | | | | | | | | | | | | | | | | | | | | | 36 | | | | | |

# Subject __________________________

| Week | Week____ | | | | | Week____ | | | | | Week____ | | | | | Week____ | | | | | Week____ | | | | | Week____ | | | | |
|---|---|---|---|---|---|---|---|---|---|---|---|---|---|---|---|---|---|---|---|---|---|---|---|---|---|---|---|---|---|---|
| Day | M | T | W | T | F | M | T | W | T | F | M | T | W | T | F | M | T | W | T | F | M | T | W | T | F | M | T | W | T | F |
| Date | | | | | | | | | | | | | | | | | | | | | | | | | | | | | | |
| Assignments or Attendance | | | | | | | | | | | | | | | | | | | | | | | | | | | | | | |
| Name | | | | | | | | | | | | | | | | | | | | | | | | | | | | | | |
| 1 | | | | | | | | | | | | | | | | | | | | | | | | | | | | | | |
| 2 | | | | | | | | | | | | | | | | | | | | | | | | | | | | | | |
| 3 | | | | | | | | | | | | | | | | | | | | | | | | | | | | | | |
| 4 | | | | | | | | | | | | | | | | | | | | | | | | | | | | | | |
| 5 | | | | | | | | | | | | | | | | | | | | | | | | | | | | | | |
| 6 | | | | | | | | | | | | | | | | | | | | | | | | | | | | | | |
| 7 | | | | | | | | | | | | | | | | | | | | | | | | | | | | | | |
| 8 | | | | | | | | | | | | | | | | | | | | | | | | | | | | | | |
| 9 | | | | | | | | | | | | | | | | | | | | | | | | | | | | | | |
| 10 | | | | | | | | | | | | | | | | | | | | | | | | | | | | | | |
| 11 | | | | | | | | | | | | | | | | | | | | | | | | | | | | | | |
| 12 | | | | | | | | | | | | | | | | | | | | | | | | | | | | | | |
| 13 | | | | | | | | | | | | | | | | | | | | | | | | | | | | | | |
| 14 | | | | | | | | | | | | | | | | | | | | | | | | | | | | | | |
| 15 | | | | | | | | | | | | | | | | | | | | | | | | | | | | | | |
| 16 | | | | | | | | | | | | | | | | | | | | | | | | | | | | | | |
| 17 | | | | | | | | | | | | | | | | | | | | | | | | | | | | | | |
| 18 | | | | | | | | | | | | | | | | | | | | | | | | | | | | | | |
| 19 | | | | | | | | | | | | | | | | | | | | | | | | | | | | | | |
| 20 | | | | | | | | | | | | | | | | | | | | | | | | | | | | | | |
| 21 | | | | | | | | | | | | | | | | | | | | | | | | | | | | | | |
| 22 | | | | | | | | | | | | | | | | | | | | | | | | | | | | | | |
| 23 | | | | | | | | | | | | | | | | | | | | | | | | | | | | | | |
| 24 | | | | | | | | | | | | | | | | | | | | | | | | | | | | | | |
| 25 | | | | | | | | | | | | | | | | | | | | | | | | | | | | | | |
| 26 | | | | | | | | | | | | | | | | | | | | | | | | | | | | | | |
| 27 | | | | | | | | | | | | | | | | | | | | | | | | | | | | | | |
| 28 | | | | | | | | | | | | | | | | | | | | | | | | | | | | | | |
| 29 | | | | | | | | | | | | | | | | | | | | | | | | | | | | | | |
| 30 | | | | | | | | | | | | | | | | | | | | | | | | | | | | | | |
| 31 | | | | | | | | | | | | | | | | | | | | | | | | | | | | | | |
| 32 | | | | | | | | | | | | | | | | | | | | | | | | | | | | | | |
| 33 | | | | | | | | | | | | | | | | | | | | | | | | | | | | | | |
| 34 | | | | | | | | | | | | | | | | | | | | | | | | | | | | | | |
| 35 | | | | | | | | | | | | | | | | | | | | | | | | | | | | | | |
| 36 | | | | | | | | | | | | | | | | | | | | | | | | | | | | | | |

# $\mathcal{P}$eriod______________________

| Week____ | | | | | Week____ | | | | | Week____ | | | | | Week____ | | | | | Week____ | | | | | | Days Present | Days Absent | Tardies | Quarter Grade | |
|---|---|---|---|---|---|---|---|---|---|---|---|---|---|---|---|---|---|---|---|---|---|---|---|---|---|---|---|---|---|---|
| M | T | W | T | F | M | T | W | T | F | M | T | W | T | F | M | T | W | T | F | M | T | W | T | F | | | | | | |
| | | | | | | | | | | | | | | | | | | | | | | | | | | | | | | |
| | | | | | | | | | | | | | | | | | | | | | | | | | 1 | | | | | |
| | | | | | | | | | | | | | | | | | | | | | | | | | 2 | | | | | |
| | | | | | | | | | | | | | | | | | | | | | | | | | 3 | | | | | |
| | | | | | | | | | | | | | | | | | | | | | | | | | 4 | | | | | |
| | | | | | | | | | | | | | | | | | | | | | | | | | 5 | | | | | |
| | | | | | | | | | | | | | | | | | | | | | | | | | 6 | | | | | |
| | | | | | | | | | | | | | | | | | | | | | | | | | 7 | | | | | |
| | | | | | | | | | | | | | | | | | | | | | | | | | 8 | | | | | |
| | | | | | | | | | | | | | | | | | | | | | | | | | 9 | | | | | |
| | | | | | | | | | | | | | | | | | | | | | | | | | 10 | | | | | |
| | | | | | | | | | | | | | | | | | | | | | | | | | 11 | | | | | |
| | | | | | | | | | | | | | | | | | | | | | | | | | 12 | | | | | |
| | | | | | | | | | | | | | | | | | | | | | | | | | 13 | | | | | |
| | | | | | | | | | | | | | | | | | | | | | | | | | 14 | | | | | |
| | | | | | | | | | | | | | | | | | | | | | | | | | 15 | | | | | |
| | | | | | | | | | | | | | | | | | | | | | | | | | 16 | | | | | |
| | | | | | | | | | | | | | | | | | | | | | | | | | 17 | | | | | |
| | | | | | | | | | | | | | | | | | | | | | | | | | 18 | | | | | |
| | | | | | | | | | | | | | | | | | | | | | | | | | 19 | | | | | |
| | | | | | | | | | | | | | | | | | | | | | | | | | 20 | | | | | |
| | | | | | | | | | | | | | | | | | | | | | | | | | 21 | | | | | |
| | | | | | | | | | | | | | | | | | | | | | | | | | 22 | | | | | |
| | | | | | | | | | | | | | | | | | | | | | | | | | 23 | | | | | |
| | | | | | | | | | | | | | | | | | | | | | | | | | 24 | | | | | |
| | | | | | | | | | | | | | | | | | | | | | | | | | 25 | | | | | |
| | | | | | | | | | | | | | | | | | | | | | | | | | 26 | | | | | |
| | | | | | | | | | | | | | | | | | | | | | | | | | 27 | | | | | |
| | | | | | | | | | | | | | | | | | | | | | | | | | 28 | | | | | |
| | | | | | | | | | | | | | | | | | | | | | | | | | 29 | | | | | |
| | | | | | | | | | | | | | | | | | | | | | | | | | 30 | | | | | |
| | | | | | | | | | | | | | | | | | | | | | | | | | 31 | | | | | |
| | | | | | | | | | | | | | | | | | | | | | | | | | 32 | | | | | |
| | | | | | | | | | | | | | | | | | | | | | | | | | 33 | | | | | |
| | | | | | | | | | | | | | | | | | | | | | | | | | 34 | | | | | |
| | | | | | | | | | | | | | | | | | | | | | | | | | 35 | | | | | |
| | | | | | | | | | | | | | | | | | | | | | | | | | 36 | | | | | |

# Notes

# Lesson Plans

*May he give you the desire of your heart*
*and make all your plans succeed.*

*Psalm 20:4*

# *Week of*______________________

| *Monday* | | | |
|---|---|---|---|

| *Tuesday* | | | |
|---|---|---|---|

| *Wednesday* | | | |
|---|---|---|---|

| *Thursday* | | | |
|---|---|---|---|

| *Friday* | | | |
|---|---|---|---|

# *Week of*______________________

| **Monday** | | | |
| --- | --- | --- | --- |
| **Tuesday** | | | |
| **Wednesday** | | | |
| **Thursday** | | | |
| **Friday** | | | |

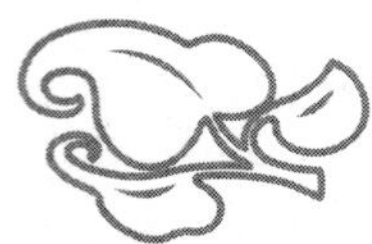

# *Week of*______________________

| Monday | | | |
|---|---|---|---|

| Tuesday | | | |
|---|---|---|---|

| Wednesday | | | |
|---|---|---|---|

| Thursday | | | |
|---|---|---|---|

| Friday | | | |
|---|---|---|---|

Be merciful to me, Lord, for I am faint.  Psalm 6:2a


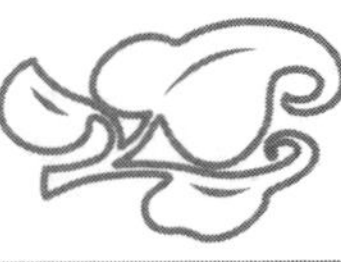

# Week of _______________

| Monday | | | |
| --- | --- | --- | --- |
| **Tuesday** | | | |
| **Wednesday** | | | |
| **Thursday** | | | |
| **Friday** | | | |

# *Week of*______________________________

| | | | |
|---|---|---|---|
| *Monday* | | | |
| *Tuesday* | | | |
| *Wednesday* | | | |
| *Thursday* | | | |
| *Friday* | | | |

# *Week of* ________________________

| *Monday* | | | |
|---|---|---|---|
| *Tuesday* | | | |
| *Wednesday* | | | |
| *Thursday* | | | |
| *Friday* | | | |

# Week of _______________

| | | | |
|---|---|---|---|
| **Monday** | | | |
| **Tuesday** | | | |
| **Wednesday** | | | |
| **Thursday** | | | |
| **Friday** | | | |

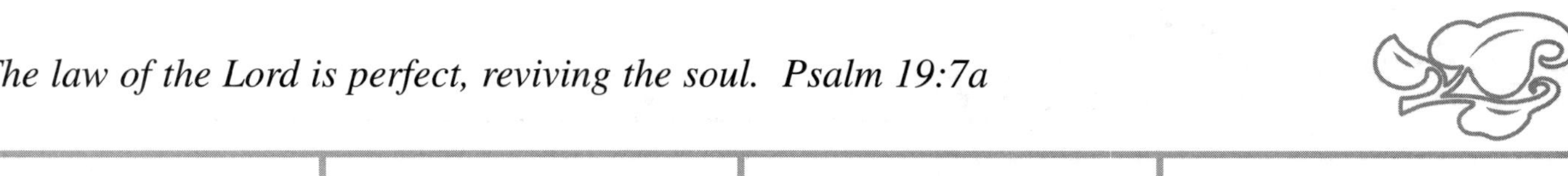

# Week of ______________________________

|  |  |  |  |
|---|---|---|---|
| **Monday** |  |  |  |
| **Tuesday** |  |  |  |
| **Wednesday** |  |  |  |
| **Thursday** |  |  |  |
| **Friday** |  |  |  |

# *Week of*________________________

| | | | |
|---|---|---|---|
| *Monday* | | | |
| *Tuesday* | | | |
| *Wednesday* | | | |
| *Thursday* | | | |
| *Friday* | | | |

# *Week of*_______________________

| *Monday* | | | |
|---|---|---|---|
| *Tuesday* | | | |
| *Wednesday* | | | |
| *Thursday* | | | |
| *Friday* | | | |

# Week of_________________________

| Monday | | | |
|---|---|---|---|
| Tuesday | | | |
| Wednesday | | | |
| Thursday | | | |
| Friday | | | |

 # Week of _______________________

| Monday | | | |
|--------|---|---|---|
| Tuesday | | | |
| Wednesday | | | |
| Thursday | | | |
| Friday | | | |

# *Week of* _______________________

| *Monday* | | | |
| --- | --- | --- | --- |
| *Tuesday* | | | |
| *Wednesday* | | | |
| *Thursday* | | | |
| *Friday* | | | |

# *Week of*_______________________

| Monday | | | |
|--------|--|--|--|
| **Tuesday** | | | |
| **Wednesday** | | | |
| **Thursday** | | | |
| **Friday** | | | |

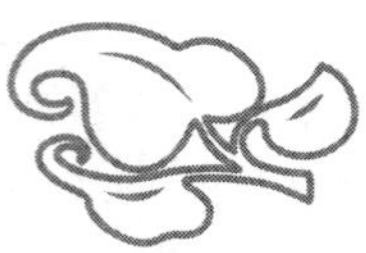

# Week of _______________________

| Monday | | | |
| --- | --- | --- | --- |
| **Tuesday** | | | |
| **Wednesday** | | | |
| **Thursday** | | | |
| **Friday** | | | |

# Week of _____________________

| Monday | | | |
|--------|--|--|--|

| Tuesday | | | |
|---------|--|--|--|

| Wednesday | | | |
|-----------|--|--|--|

| Thursday | | | |
|----------|--|--|--|

| Friday | | | |
|--------|--|--|--|

# Week of _______________________

| Monday | | | |
|---|---|---|---|

| Tuesday | | | |
|---|---|---|---|

| Wednesday | | | |
|---|---|---|---|

| Thursday | | | |
|---|---|---|---|

| Friday | | | |
|---|---|---|---|

*I call on the Lord in my distress, and he answers me.  Psalm 120:1*

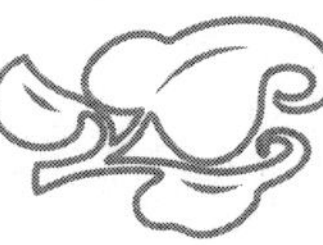

# Week of ___________________

| Monday | | | |
|--------|--|--|--|
| **Tuesday** | | | |
| **Wednesday** | | | |
| **Thursday** | | | |
| **Friday** | | | |

# *Week of*_______________________

| | | | |
|---|---|---|---|
| *Monday* | | | |
| *Tuesday* | | | |
| *Wednesday* | | | |
| *Thursday* | | | |
| *Friday* | | | |

# *Week of* _______________________

| *Monday* | | | |
|---|---|---|---|
| *Tuesday* | | | |
| *Wednesday* | | | |
| *Thursday* | | | |
| *Friday* | | | |

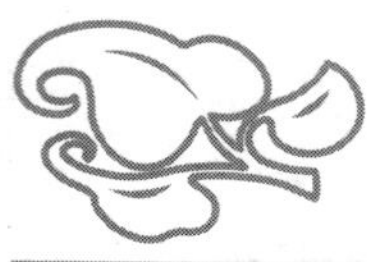

# *Week of*_______________________

| *Monday* | | | |
|---|---|---|---|
| *Tuesday* | | | |
| *Wednesday* | | | |
| *Thursday* | | | |
| *Friday* | | | |

# *Week of* _______________________

| Monday |  |  |  |
|--------|--|--|--|

| Tuesday |  |  |  |
|---------|--|--|--|

| Wednesday |  |  |  |
|-----------|--|--|--|

| Thursday |  |  |  |
|----------|--|--|--|

| Friday |  |  |  |
|--------|--|--|--|

# *Week of*______________________

| **Monday** | | | |
| --- | --- | --- | --- |
| **Tuesday** | | | |
| **Wednesday** | | | |
| **Thursday** | | | |
| **Friday** | | | |

*Be patient, bearing with one another in love. Ephesians 4:2b*

| | | | |
|---|---|---|---|
| | | | |
| | | | |
| | | | |
| | | | |
| | | | |

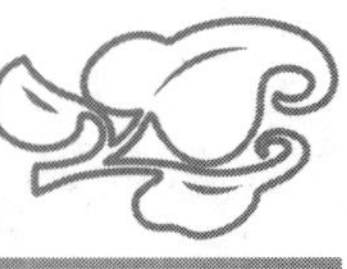

# *Week of*_______________________

| *Monday* | | | |
|---|---|---|---|

| *Tuesday* | | | |
|---|---|---|---|

| *Wednesday* | | | |
|---|---|---|---|

| *Thursday* | | | |
|---|---|---|---|

| *Friday* | | | |
|---|---|---|---|

# *Week of* _______________________

| **Monday** | | | |
| --- | --- | --- | --- |
| **Tuesday** | | | |
| **Wednesday** | | | |
| **Thursday** | | | |
| **Friday** | | | |

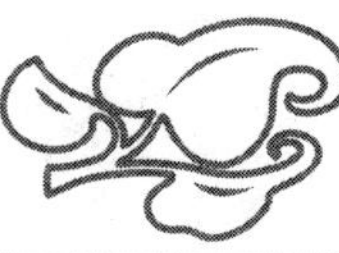

# *Week of* _______________________

| *Monday* | | | |
|---|---|---|---|
| *Tuesday* | | | |
| *Wednesday* | | | |
| *Thursday* | | | |
| *Friday* | | | |

# *Week of*______________________

| Monday | | | |
|---|---|---|---|
| **Tuesday** | | | |
| **Wednesday** | | | |
| **Thursday** | | | |
| **Friday** | | | |

# *Week of* _______________________

| *Monday* | | | |
| --- | --- | --- | --- |
| *Tuesday* | | | |
| *Wednesday* | | | |
| *Thursday* | | | |
| *Friday* | | | |

# *Week of* ___________________________

| **Monday** | | | |
| --- | --- | --- | --- |
| **Tuesday** | | | |
| **Wednesday** | | | |
| **Thursday** | | | |
| **Friday** | | | |

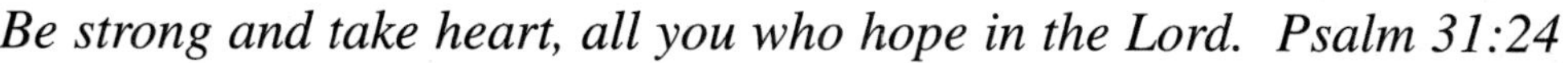

*Be strong and take heart, all you who hope in the Lord.  Psalm 31:24*

# Week of _______________

| Monday | | | |
|---|---|---|---|
| **Tuesday** | | | |
| **Wednesday** | | | |
| **Thursday** | | | |
| **Friday** | | | |

# Week of _______________

| Monday | | | |
|---|---|---|---|
| **Tuesday** | | | |
| **Wednesday** | | | |
| **Thursday** | | | |
| **Friday** | | | |

# *Week of* ___________________

| Monday | | | |
|---|---|---|---|
| **Tuesday** | | | |
| **Wednesday** | | | |
| **Thursday** | | | |
| **Friday** | | | |

# *Week of*___________________

| *Monday* | | | |
|---|---|---|---|
| *Tuesday* | | | |
| *Wednesday* | | | |
| *Thursday* | | | |
| *Friday* | | | |

# *Week of*_______________________

| *Monday* | | | |
|---|---|---|---|
| *Tuesday* | | | |
| *Wednesday* | | | |
| *Thursday* | | | |
| *Friday* | | | |

# Week of ______________________

| Monday | | | |
| --- | --- | --- | --- |
| **Tuesday** | | | |
| **Wednesday** | | | |
| **Thursday** | | | |
| **Friday** | | | |

# Week of _______________________

| Monday | | | |
| Tuesday | | | |
| Wednesday | | | |
| Thursday | | | |
| Friday | | | |

# Week of _______________________

| Monday | | | |
| --- | --- | --- | --- |
| **Tuesday** | | | |
| **Wednesday** | | | |
| **Thursday** | | | |
| **Friday** | | | |

# Week of _______________

| Monday | | | |
|---|---|---|---|
| Tuesday | | | |
| Wednesday | | | |
| Thursday | | | |
| Friday | | | |

# *Week of*____________________

| Monday | | | |
|--------|--|--|--|
| **Tuesday** | | | |
| **Wednesday** | | | |
| **Thursday** | | | |
| **Friday** | | | |

# *Week of*_____________________

| Monday | | | |
| --- | --- | --- | --- |
| | | | |
| **Tuesday** | | | |
| | | | |
| **Wednesday** | | | |
| | | | |
| **Thursday** | | | |
| | | | |
| **Friday** | | | |

# *Week of*_______________________

| Monday | | | |
| --- | --- | --- | --- |
| **Tuesday** | | | |
| **Wednesday** | | | |
| **Thursday** | | | |
| **Friday** | | | |

# Notes